Miracle at the Mall

The True Story of Landen Hoffmann, Who Survived Being Thrown from a 39-Foot-High Balcony at the Largest Mall in America

Kari Hoffmann

Miracle at the Mall

Copyright © 2025 by Kari Hoffmann

Editing by Holly Crawshaw and Chris McKinney (calledwriters.com)

Portrait (right side) cover photo by: Kenny Kim Photography (kennykim.com). Same photo also used in About the Author section.

All rights reserved. No portion of this book may be reproduced, stored in a retrieval system, or transmitted in any form or by any means except for brief quotations in critical reviews or articles, without the prior written permission of the publisher.

Scripture quotations marked NIV taken from the Holy Bible, *NEW INTERNATIONAL VERSION*,® NIV.® Copyright © 1973, 1978, 1984, 2011 by Biblica, Inc.™ Used by permission. All rights reserved worldwide.

Scripture quotations marked NKJV are taken from the New King James Version®. Copyright © 1982 by Thomas Nelson. Used by permission. All rights reserved.

Scripture quotations marked ESV are from the ESV® Bible (The Holy Bible, English Standard Version®), copyright © 2001 by Crossway, a publishing ministry of Good News Publishers. Used by permission. All rights reserved.

Scripture quotations marked NLT are taken from the Holy Bible, New Living Translation, copyright © 1996, 2004, 2007 by Tyndale House Foundation. Used by permission of Tyndale House Publishers, Inc., Carol Stream, IL 60188. All rights reserved.

Scripture quotations marked AMP are taken from the Amplified Bible, Copyright © 2015 by The Lockman Foundation. Used by permission.

Scripture quotations marked ERV are taken from the HOLY BIBLE: EASY-TO-READ VERSION © 2001 by World Bible Translation Center, Inc. and used by permission.

Scripture quotations marked CEB are taken from the COMMON ENGLISH BIBLE. © Copyright 2011 COMMON ENGLISH BIBLE. All rights reserved. Used by permission.

Scripture quotations marked NCV are taken from the New Century Version®. Copyright © 2005 by Thomas Nelson. Used by permission. All rights reserved.

Published by Called Writers Christian Publishing, LLC

Tuscaloosa, Alabama

Contents

1. The Warning — 5
2. Preparation — 9
3. The Dream — 17
4. Fighting Against Pure Evil — 21
5. Breakthroughs in the Chaos — 27
6. The Strength of a Dad — 33
7. What Just Happened? — 37
8. The Prognosis — 43
9. Finding Rest — 49
10. Staying Focused amid Book and TV Offers, and International News Coverage — 53
11. A Chance at Life — 61
12. A Special Place in My Heart — 65
13. A Place of Peace — 69
14. Anointing with Oil — 73
15. Another Attack on Landen's Life — 83
16. Resurrection Power — 89
17. Waiting — 95
18. Controlling the Narrative — 101
19. Not Today, Satan! — 107
20. Surprising the Doctors — 111
21. Worldwide Prayer, Love, & Support — 117
22. When Hope Wears a Jersey — 129
23. Jesus Loves Me — 135
24. Intense Pain — 141
25. The Man Who Did This — 147
26. The Power of Hope — 151
27. Finding Strength — 155
28. Outlasting the Enemy — 161
29. Tapping Out — 167
30. Breakthrough — 173
31. A Hidden Miracle — 179
32. The Sun Is Still Shining — 183

33. Holding On	187
34. Nurse Heroes	191
35. Freedom	195
36. The Trial Is Over	199
37. Not All Angels Have Wings	207
Afterword	215
About the Author	223

Chapter 1

The Warning

CHILLS.

Driving up to the largest mall in America, I followed my usual route along the north side, past an impressive glass hotel standing a dozen stories tall. Landen, my five-year-old son, happily colored in the backseat of the SUV, smearing his water bottle with markers that rubbed off on his hands like a kaleidoscope.

As I edged toward a parking ramp, I felt a sudden, overwhelming sense that something was wrong.

We shouldn't be here, I thought, the chills running through my body. It didn't make any sense to me at all, so I tried to write it off as irrational.

In a flurry of texts earlier that morning, I had coordinated our outing with another mom, Betsy, and her young son, Will, who was a preschool classmate of Landen's. We trekked to the mall together in separate vehicles, sloshing through the leftovers of a mid-April blizzard that ended only hours before.

My skin rose in goosebumps again, but it had nothing to do with the cold. I felt like we needed protection. *From what, Lord?* I prayed. The feeling gnawed at my instincts, urging me to be cautious. *Lord, protect us today,* I prayed.

The mall is fun, I reminded myself, trying to shake off the worry. Just twenty minutes from home, our family frequently visited the mall to eat, shop, and ride rides at the Nickelodeon Universe amusement park at the mall's center. During long Minnesota winters, the mall's three miles of indoor walkways were a pleasant escape.

I thought back on the parent-teacher conference I attended at Landen's preschool that morning. This final conference before the end of the year was terrific. Landen worked well, got along quickly, and never created problems. My baby was on his way to kindergarten, and I wanted to celebrate him with a trip to one of the big kids stores at the mall.

I was overwhelmed with gratitude for my little boy. I rarely called my husband during the workday, but after the conference, I had to tell Dave how proud we should be of Landen.

Parking the car, I smiled and waved at Betsy, who parked right beside me. She and I had been friends for the year and a half our boys had been together in preschool. With time to kill before the stores opened, I waved for her and Will to climb into our vehicle.

Landen and Will jumped to the far back of the SUV, laughing as they pulled a blanket over their heads.

"It is such a relief to get out of the house," Betsy said, pushing the hair from her face with a frazzled look. "The dishwasher flooded and completely ruined the floor. I've got to find someone to come out and fix it."

Struggling to hear Betsy over the boys' giggling and screaming, I shushed them.

Betsy went on talking about finding the right contractor, but the chilled feeling lingered in my chest, preventing me from fully engaging in the conversation. I wondered if I should listen more to the feeling, but I pushed it away. *We're here to have fun*, I reminded myself, shoving the sense of dread back down.

Ten minutes before the mall was scheduled to open, we emptied the car and headed toward the entrance.

While the mall slowly came to life around us, I couldn't ignore the persistent unease that tingled in the depths of my being. The disturbed feeling grew as we approached the doors. I knew we needed protection from something. Under my breath, I prayed, "Lord, let angels go before us to protect us wherever we go."

I had been praying under my breath since childhood, but this prayer felt different from any prayer I had ever prayed. It just came out of me. As I prayed, my dread subsided. I felt like whatever danger was looming, God had the situation covered. I was ready to move on, so I let it go. *I'm done*, I thought. *Now, I'm going to have a good day.* I was ready to see the boys letting loose and having fun!

The boys ran ahead, so excited they bumped into a cleaning cart pushed by a mall employee.

"I'm so sorry!" I said, pulling ahead to try and grab hold of Landen.

"No worries!" she said, smiling. "I have a rambunctious boy of my own."

The coffee shops were opening, and handfuls of people moved around the mall. We were the first customers in line, and after our stop the boys ran ahead. "Landen!" I kept saying. "Come back!" I was struggling to shake the disquieting feeling from earlier, so I wanted him close to me.

The kids store we were heading for was on the third floor of a large atrium at the northwest corner of the mall. The atrium was ringed by balconies, with large skylights above, creating a warm welcome. The store still wasn't open, and no one was in the immediate area, but the boys knew that a particular restaurant was just around the corner, with a moat and robot alligator out front that made steam. They ran that way, heading straight for the rocks around the moat, a favorite play area for them.

A big sign said not to climb on the rocks, but we had eaten at the café often enough to know the sign didn't seem to matter to anyone. The boys stepped up and leaned over for a better look at the alligator, protesting that it wasn't running its usual steam.

A man walked up and leaned over with them. He was a nice-looking younger guy without a winter coat, dressed in a bright white t-shirt. He looked like he was there to work. *How about getting the alligator going?* I thought, assuming he was a mall employee.

Betsy and I stood nearby chatting, watching the boys to make sure they didn't fall on the rocks.

The man looked my way and smiled, showing faint dimples. I watched him lean over to Will and whisper something. I couldn't hear what he said, but the boys giggled.

I stepped closer, not yet feeling the impending disaster. My only thought was that maybe he needed the boys to move.

"Excuse me, do you want the boys off the rocks?" I asked.

The man smiled. "No, no. You're fine," he said, stretching his arm straight ahead and wagging his hand—a gesture to make it clear they weren't causing trouble.

"Do you work here?" I asked. "Are you going to turn the alligator on?"

He smiled again. He made me feel like I could trust him. I was right next to him. Just an arm's length away. In fact, when he said again it was okay for the boys to be there, I took a step back.

Little did I know, darkness lurked beneath that smile.

"You intended to harm me, but God intended it for good to accomplish what is now being done, saving many lives."

— GENESIS 50:20 NIV

God, guard me in life's darkest moments. I trust that Your eyes are wide open even when the world intends to harm. You watch over me without fail.

Chapter 2

Preparation

That day at the mall was not the first time in my life I would encounter evil.

It was a few weeks after my last day of fifth grade, seemingly just another summer night filled with dreams of carefree days and endless sunshine. But darkness descended upon my home that night, shattering my sense of security and innocence.

I awoke around 4 or 5 am to see my older sister and younger brother standing by my bed. Lurking behind them was an adult I had never seen, holding a handgun. A cloth concealed his face, his intentions hidden in the shadows.

Hours earlier, my dad was preparing my sister for a big softball game, tossing a ball in the backyard. Unbeknownst to us all, a simple oversight left the garage door open. In the wee hours of the morning, the intruder, who had been scouring the neighborhood on his bicycle for houses to loot, seized the opportunity and slipped through the open garage, invading our sanctuary.

Inside our home, the intruder rifled through my mom's purse but was unsatisfied with his findings. A twisted determination possessed him as he wrapped a small tablecloth around his face and silently ascended the stairs.

He entered my little brother's room first. Matt, only nine years old, awoke to the barrel of a gun and the chilling command to get up. The same scene repeated itself in my sister's room, where Mandy, thirteen at the time, experienced her worst nightmare come to life. Through it all, the intruder's voice, cold and menacing, warned us against screaming.

My bedroom was next. Mandy shook me awake. I had barely blinked my blurry eyes when the intruder pushed us toward the last bedroom, where Mandy obeyed the man's command to wake our parents.

Our mom responded first, thinking, *Is that a man in the darkness? Holding a gun on my children?*

She jumped out of bed. "What do you want?" she questioned. Her voice brimmed with both defiance and compassion.

No answer.

"Steve!" my mom said to my dad. It was the morning of their twentieth anniversary, and Dad had scheduled a day off. Disoriented and caught off guard, yet aware of the grave circumstance, his first instinct was to pray.

Mom attempted to reason with the intruder, offering help if he needed it, and his eyes darted with uncertainty. We were all herded into the hallway, down the staircase, and into the first-floor family room, where we sat together on the couch, a family held captive by fear and the unyielding presence of a gun.

Mom persisted in questioning, striving to stall for time and hopefully understand the intruder's motives. "What do you need? Why are you here? What are you going to do? Do you want money? Can we at least get dressed? I need my glasses. Please, let me retrieve my glasses."

The intruder still was not responding very much. He shook his head "no" and grunted a lot. When he did talk to give us orders, it was usually short, in a low sort of voice—almost like he didn't want us to remember any details about him, including his voice. He also had the tablecloth draped over most of his face, and hanging down to his waist the whole time.

As Mom continued talking, Dad said, "Kids, pray! Keep praying!" Dad prayed in his big dad voice. The rest of us joined in loudly enough that our noise caused confusion and hesitation in the intruder's mind. His composure began to crumble amidst our collective resilience.

He moved us from the family room to the garage, where three vehicles were parked—Dad's big work van, a family conversion van, and a giant Buick gifted to our family when my great aunt passed away.

Upon arriving at the garage, the intruder demanded the keys to the Buick, the vehicle he had set his sights on. "Where are the keys?" he growled, his impatience betraying an escalating agitation.

"I don't know," Mom replied firmly, determination laced in her words. "We never drive that car." It wasn't true, but she needed to stall for more precious seconds and devise a way out of this nightmare.

The man forced us to walk through the maze of cars—kids in front, then Mom, and finally, Dad, with the gun to his back.

I was a little too helpful when I got to the car and quickly retrieved the keys. "Here they are!" I said.

Amidst the tension, my gaze fell upon a roll of CAUTION tape, an eerily familiar vibrant yellow. It was something Dad had to use in his fire extinguisher business, but at this moment, it brought foreboding images to mind.

A gut feeling alerted Mom to the intruder's intentions, and she drew a firm line. "We are not getting into that trunk!" she declared, her defiance providing a glimmer of hope amidst the engulfing darkness.

This momentary distraction allowed Dad to regain his bearings. He turned around, seizing an opportunity to strike back. With a surge of determination, he lunged and clutched the gun barrel with both hands, forcing the intruder's arm upward.

Chaos erupted.

A loud gunshot echoed through the garage, shattering the quiet of the night.

"Mandy, call 911!" Mom's voice pierced through the chaos, a command amidst panic. "Kari, Matthew, get back in the house!"

Dad fought with an indomitable strength, pummeling the intruder until he subdued him, the intruder's power diminished by the pure force of a father protecting his family. After calling 911, Mandy grabbed one of Dad's fire extinguishers, intending to spray the man in the face. This actually could have been very effective in a sense, as the chemical used in fire extinguishers displaces all the oxygen from the air. A person getting a direct spray to the face would be gasping desperately, unable to get any oxygen.

However, it might have also caused Dad to be unable to breathe given his close proximity to the intruder. So it was likely divine intervention that Mandy could not figure out how to pull the pin and spray the chemical—something she had certainly been instructed by Dad to be able to do.

The wounded intruder, now pinned beneath Dad's relentless blows, was held in check until the police arrived. As the dust settled, we learned the man's true nature—a 27-year-old previously convicted of a similar crime. He had spent time in prison, but the system had failed to prevent him from wreaking havoc once more.

The man quickly admitted his plan. He was going to tie us up, force us into the trunk, and make my mom drive to an ATM to withdraw cash. His nine-millimeter Glock was loaded with 17 bullets. After the first shot, his gun had jammed. The police told us this was a miracle, as Glocks are renowned for their reliability, and there was no apparent obstruction inside the gun. We believe this happened because of our prayers. He was charged with burglary, kidnapping, and aggravated robbery.

MIRACLE AT THE MALL

State of Minnesota County of HENNEPIN DISTRICT Court

CCT	SECTION/Subdivision	U.O.C	COC
1	609.582,1(b);609.11	B1114	N
2	609.582,1(c);609.11	B1111	N
3	609.222;609.11, PM'92	A2326	N
4	609.25(1)(2),2(2);609.11	K3226	N
5	609.222;609.11	A2326	N
6	609.25,1(2),2(2);609.11	K3226	N

CITY ATTY FILE NO: 92-2044
CONTROLLING AGENCY NO: 0270300
CONTROL NO: 92014270
COURT CASE NO:
DATE FILED:

Complaint
SUMMONS
WARRANT
XXX ORDER OF DETENTION

State of Minnesota
PLAINTIFF
VS.
XXX FELONY
GROSS MISDEMEANOR

NAME: first, middle, last
[REDACTED]
92048371
Date of Birth [REDACTED]
SJIS COMPLAINT NUMBER
27-11-J-166496
HENNEPIN CITY

DEFENDANT.

COMPLAINT

The Complainant, being duly sworn, makes complaint to the above-named Court and states that there is probable cause to believe that the Defendant committed the following offense(s). The complainant states that the following facts establish PROBABLE CAUSE.

Your Complainant, Detective George Moore of the Brooklyn Park Police Department, has investigated the facts and circumstances of this case by reviewing the reports of fellow officers, by interviewing victims of the crimes, and by reviewing the interview of the defendant.

Complainant has learned that on June 23, 1992, at approximately 5:00 a.m., Brooklyn Park police were called to a home at 3243 Berwick Knoll in Brooklyn Park, Hennepin County, Minnesota, regarding a burglary in progress at that address. Upon arrival, officers found the family members who reside at that address in the garage and observed that the adult male of the family had an Asian male pinned to the floor and was holding him down for police officers. Officers took the Asian male, later identified as [REDACTED] defendant herein, into custody at that time.

Complainant has spoken with each of the five family members who reside at the above address and has learned the following: The home located at 3243 Berwick Knoll is a single family home with an attached garage. The garage has one double door and one single door, containing three garage stalls. On the evening of June 22, 1992, at approximately 9:30 p.m., family members came into the home, but neglected to close the single garage door for the night. The family later determined that the service door which enters into the home was also left unlocked that evening. Members of the family went to bed at approximately 11:00 p.m. that evening.

At approximately 5:00 a.m. on June 23, 1992, the youngest member of the family, M.H., dob [REDACTED], age 8, was awakened by a man who was armed with a gun and was in his bedroom and told him to get up. The man, later identified as [REDACTED], defendant herein, told M.H. to be

THEREFORE, Complainant requests that said Defendant, subject to bail or conditions of release be:
(1) arrested or that other lawful steps be taken to obtain defendant's appearance in court; or
(2) detained, if already in custody, pending further proceedings;
and that said Defendant otherwise be dealt with according to law.

COMPLAINANT'S NAME: George Moore
COMPLAINANT'S SIGNATURE: George W. Moore #(60)

Being duly authorized to prosecute the offense(s) charged, I hereby approve this Complaint.

DATE: June 24, 1992
PROSECUTING ATTORNEY'S SIGNATURE: Mary E. Hannon

PROSECUTING ATTORNEY: Mary E. Hannon:ks
NAME/TITLE: ASSISTANT COUNTY ATTORNEY
ADDRESS/TELEPHONE: C2100 GOVERNMENT CENTER
348-3508/175699

FORM B-1

Police report first page

> quiet and then directed him to go into the next bedroom and wake up his sister. The defendant pointed the gun at M.H. while directing him. The defendant and M.H. then went into the bedroom of A.H., dob ▓▓▓, age 13, and A.H. reports waking up and seeing a man pointing a gun at her. The defendant told her to get up and be quiet and directed her into the next bedroom, which was her sister's room. The two children and the defendant then went into the third child's room and woke that child up. K.H., dob ▓▓▓, age 11, told police that she was awakened by her brother and her sister and the defendant who was standing there with a gun and was telling her to get up. All of the children noticed that the defendant had some kind of mask or handkerchief over his face at the time he woke them up. The defendant ordered the children not to scream and then directed them into their parents' bedroom and told them to wake up their parents.
>
> The mother in the home, an adult female, K.D.H., dob ▓▓▓, woke up and saw the defendant standing at her bed with her three children. She also noticed a scarf tied over the defendant's face and saw that he had a gun in his hand and was pointing it at her and her husband. The father in the family, S.H., dob ▓▓▓ then woke up to see the defendant pointing a gun at him and telling him to get up. The defendant then directed the entire family, all still dressed in their pajamas, to a downstairs family room in the home. The defendant demanded the keys to one of the cars in the garage from the family and the family told the defendant they did not know where the keys were and that they were possibly in the car in the garage. The defendant then forced the entire family to go out into the garage where the cars were parked. The defendant then directed the family to close the garage door that was open and ordered them to find the car keys for him. One of the children then left the garage area to find the car keys. While the family was in the garage with the defendant, S.H. observed that the defendant had a roll of yellow adhesive tape which had previously been in the family garage in his hands. The defendant told the family to open the trunk of one of the cars and told the family members to get into the trunk of the car. At that point S.H., dob ▓▓▓, took the opportunity to grab the gun which the defendant was holding in his hand and a struggle began. During that struggle, a shot was fired and the bullet missed the people in the garage and went through a vehicle in the garage and through the garage wall. K.D.H., dob ▓▓▓, also entered the struggle between her husband and the defendant, in an effort to take the gun from the defendant. During that struggle, K.D.H. was bitten in the thigh by the defendant. S.H. sustained powder burns to his hand from the gun. S.H. was eventually able to get the defendant to release his grip on the gun and K.D.H. got the gun and threw it into one of the vehicles. During the struggle, one of the children called 9-1-1 from a phone in the garage and another of the children ran to a neighbor and called 9-1-1. Police responded to the scene immediately and, as stated above, apprehended the defendant in the garage where he was being held by S.H.
>
> The family later determined that approximately $200 in cash had been stolen from K.D.H.'s purse which was in the family home at the time of the defendant's entry. K.D.H. had been at the bank the day before this burglary and knew the denominations of the bills she had in her purse. No

Police report second page

There were a lot of news reports, as well as magazine and newspaper articles, about the incident. Some of them even openly covered the faith aspects of the situation, with one article quoting my dad as saying that he relied on his "personal relationship with Jesus Christ" to get through the incident. *Woman's World* magazine, which had many millions of weekly readers, did a full page write-up about a dream my mother had and how God had used it to prepare her for what happened (more on that in the next chapter). The headline, laid over top of a photo they took of our family, read, "Kathy's dream saved her family." All of us had our pictures in multiple newspapers, and there was even one image of me pointing at the bullet hole that was made when the gun discharged.

It probably came across as a very happy ending, and in many respects, it was. However, my mom saw how the home invasion affected us kids. In a victim impact letter to the court, she wrote, "My children have suffered nightmares and many sleepless nights. We now must deal with fear in our everyday lives. They no longer feel safe and secure in their beds. Our whole family has to deal with the fear of being vulnerable in our home. This incident has changed our lives forever."

> "Be strong and courageous. Do not be afraid or terrified because of them, for the LORD your God goes with you; he will never leave nor forsake you."
>
> — Deuteronomy 31:6 NIV

God, You will never leave me or let me down. I will, therefore, choose to be strong and courageous. I will put aside my terror and trust in You.

Chapter 3

The Dream

When my mom woke to see a stranger standing by her bed, pointing a gun at her children, she had already seen the scene play out. Roughly a year before the home invasion, my mom had dreamed of a man standing in her bedroom and holding her children at gunpoint.

She found the dream very vivid, and the entire next day, she felt a sense of terror about it. She began to think through how she would respond if she were ever in that type of situation. She would need to stay calm and make rational decisions.

When the intruder appeared that night, she immediately recognized this as the man and the situation from her dream. That insight helped her stay calm during a terrifying moment, and she later realized the dream was a gift from God to keep fear from consuming her in that moment. She did exactly what she had envisioned, which was to stay calm and think rationally about how best to navigate the situation.

The impact of this dream cannot be overstated. God worked through it to save our lives, and at the time, Mom was able to share that testimony and give glory to Jesus. One newspaper even did a full page writeup about mom's dream and how God had used it to prepare her and help her to know what to do in the situation.

Now, God had done the same thing for me. He had given me the preparation I needed to respond in faith when facing the most difficult trial of my life.

Bad things happen. We don't always understand why. But we can be sure God is with us. Just as my mom's dream steeled her for a home invasion, my experience of that childhood incident readied me as much as anything could for the horrifying event I would later face as an adult—and also for the months and years ahead.

In time, my fears from the home invasion faded into healthy habits. I think about home safety. I make sure doors are locked. I internalized three lessons about what to do when facing evil: Pray. Fight. Trust.

Pray: Talk to God about all my needs.

Fight: Do my part with all my strength.

Trust: Focus on God with all my heart.

God watches over us without fail. He expects us to act. He invites each of us to have a childlike faith in Him. Believe. Don't go down the path of doubt. One doubt leads to another, which leads to fear.

I was raised knowing these truths.

Every night, Dad read us Bible stories and taught us to pray. My siblings and I would pile into a bed—usually mine—where we squirmed, poked, and pushed each other to the floor. There was plenty of laughter. But Dad was persistent, whether the outcome was us praying our short prayers or just giving a simple "Amen" at the end of his prayer.

Every Saturday, Sunday, and Wednesday night, we were at church. It was fun because we were with friends in a separate service for children. Because I was there all the time, I got the job of writing name tags, even though I had no idea how to spell.

Although I would have liked to stand up front with a microphone, I was too silly. So, I joined the puppet team. Starting in elementary school, I worked with other kids, practicing skits on Wednesdays and performing for children's church on the weekends.

A few years later, it felt natural to go to college to become a teacher like my mom, my uncle, and my cousin Katie.

A group of guys at college convinced me to go out with a guy they said was a hockey player. My dad and brother were both hockey players. The guy my friends wanted me to date went to another school, and he supposedly was injured, which meant he didn't have practice.

As it turned out, there was no injury, and Dave didn't even play hockey. But he was brilliant, kind, and outgoing.

After Dave and I married, I began teaching at a school connected to the church where I grew up. Staff and students met weekly for worship. I was always pretty quiet, even though I was in an environment that welcomed and encouraged prayer with our fellow teachers. Teachers would pray for each other, for the school, the church, the nation, loved ones, and for students. In all of our meetings, I never prayed out loud. I felt far more comfortable praying in my heart while others spoke up.

After I started teaching, I was ready to move on to the next part of my plan: becoming a mom. After years of struggling to get pregnant, Dave and I had twins through in vitro fertilization (IVF). I was so excited to be a mom. I quit my job to stay at home with Haley and Haden.

Two years later, we were devastated when another attempt to get pregnant failed, leaving us with one last fertilized egg. The doctor doubted the embryo would implant. In the simple description of our fertility expert, it was "ugly." Despite his prediction, that "ugly" embryo brought us a baby in perfect health, Landen.

The birth of Landen felt miraculous, and we were grateful. Life was good, but it was challenging.

During preschool, Haley withdrew from everyone except her twin and a couple of playmates. She was diagnosed with developmental delays, then autism. Haden, in contrast, was a fireball, always going as fast as he could, as hard as he could. He was always wondering, thinking, and asking why. Landen wrestled with his siblings, but he was a happy boy, thrilled to be starting baseball and hockey like his big brother.

On top of juggling three active young children, I felt awful physically and emotionally. I learned I had an autoimmune disease that likely caused our difficulties getting pregnant. Bringing my newly revealed condition under control required painstaking trial and error. In the midst of it all, I felt disconnected from my husband. He was an active dad, but his role at work frequently took him on the road. We were drifting apart.

I didn't know where my life was headed. I was crying out to God. I needed a change.

Little did I know how drastically our lives would change in such a short time.

> "'For I know the plans I have for you,' declares the LORD, 'plans to prosper you and not to harm you, plans to give you hope and a future.'"
>
> — JEREMIAH 29:11 NIV

God, I trust You through every up and down of life. I know Your plans for me are good. You give me hope and a future!

Chapter 4

Fighting Against Pure Evil

I wish I'd never stepped back.

Maybe if I had decided to talk to the man a little more. Maybe if I had stayed closer to Landen. But I didn't. I relaxed. Let my guard down. And in a shocking instant, the man snatched Landen and fled towards the edge of the third-floor balcony.

My heart stopped, frozen with terror, as I watched him callously throw my precious boy over the edge. The world seemed to shatter around me as my piercing scream echoed through the atrium.

The man fell as he threw Landen and was on the ground, trying to get up. For a second, I saw his white Nikes scrambling.

I was still screaming.

I initially ran in the wrong direction, thinking I was taking the fastest way to the first floor, nearly 40 feet below. I made it about 10 feet before remembering the escalator was on the opposite side of the atrium.

I ran back past Betsy and Will without seeing them. She screamed for help while calling out, "White shirt! White Nikes!" so the man couldn't get away unnoticed.

I reached the escalators and ran down the two long flights, skipping steps on the way. With everything in me, I screamed, "Somebody threw my baby!"

People started gathering along the glass and metal railings that circled the atrium.

At the bottom of the final escalator, I turned left.

"Where is my baby?" I shouted.

A woman in front of me didn't speak. Her eyes were wide open, and her face was pale and sober as she pointed with one finger.

Landen was behind me.

I reached the mall's ground floor, where an ashen woman pointed the way to Landen behind me. As I spun around, my gaze fixated on my little boy, lying motionless and so small on the cold, hard floor tiles. All alone. I ran to him and kneeled by his head. My impulse was to scoop up my baby in my arms. I grabbed his head.

"No! Don't touch him!" a voice near the escalator screamed. "You have to put him down!"

I came to learn later that her name was Linda, and due to the snow, she was taking the day off from treating her physical therapy clients. She was the first person to reach Landen and I on the ground floor. She didn't know what to do, so she asked God to help her and then started chest compressions the best she could until help arrived.

I am not going to lose Landen, I thought. *He is going to live.* I knew the only One who could help me was God. I cried out, "God, save my baby! Save my baby!"

I looked up and saw people staring from the second and third-floor balconies. I yelled at them, "Stop staring! Please start praying! Pray! Pray!"

I prayed aloud and then said, "Devil, take your hands off of Landen!"

I knew we were in a battle for my son's life, and I was going to fight. He was not going to take Landen that day!

Two nurses, Kimberly (not her real name) and Jessica, appeared and immediately took over chest compressions on my little boy.

They rarely visited the mall, but that day, Kimberly and Jessica were there to return an item at a store on the second level. When they arrived at the shop, it was closed. The owner emerged and said their HVAC system was acting up, and he asked if they could give him ten minutes to address the problem.

So, Kimberly and Jessica found themselves in an unexpected wait. If the store had been open, they would have gone inside. If it had been closed any longer, they would have walked away.

God stationed these two children's hospital nurses perfectly in that specific location. They were at the right spot at the right time to hear me screaming, "Somebody threw my baby!" as I ran down the escalator. They looked over the balcony rail and saw Landen. While other people scattered at the commotion, they ran toward Landen. They knew how to save lives. They knew they could help.

They ran down the escalator towards us, ready to confront the precipice between life and death where Landen teetered. He had stopped breathing. I would find out later on that there was no heartbeat when the two nurses first found him. My child, for that timeless moment, was gone.

But then—"We have a heartbeat!" The nurses' words were a sweet melody, and I echoed them, a fierce affirmation amidst the fear. "Yes! We have a heartbeat!"

"He took a breath!"

As they relayed this miracle, hope surged with my echo. "Yes! He's breathing!"

I rooted for Landen out loud, assuring him that he was doing wonderfully and breathing—a beacon of life was all that mattered. I shouted, "Good job, Landen! You have a heartbeat! Good job, Landen! You're breathing!"

Jessica continued working on Landen even after the EMTs arrived.

I glanced upward once more, and a man on the second level stood out to me. With urgency and desperation, I again begged everyone around for prayers, and that's when this stranger pointed directly at me. He silently assured me, saying, "I've got you." I couldn't help but believe he was an angel sent to be on my team, fervently praying for Landen's life.

Jessica stayed with me as we stood watching the EMTs work on

Landen. She grabbed my shoulders, saying, "What do you need? Whatever you need, I'll do it." Her support calmed me. I asked for water because I could barely breathe. I couldn't swallow from all the shouting.

Time passed in slow motion. I was in fight mode. I was still shouting. I peed my pants. I had so much liquid in me, but I wasn't going to leave Landen for any reason, and definitely not something as trivial as using the bathroom.

Suddenly, there was a stretcher. Jessica stuck by my side while Landen was delicately moved. As my boy was wheeled down the hallway, I walked beside him. People in the hallway stopped to watch. I was furious at them because they were just standing there.

"Pray!" I yelled. I needed to hear prayers.

Betsy appeared as we passed through a door to the outside of the mall. I yelled to her, "Call Dave! Somebody call Dave!"

When the first responders loaded Landen into an ambulance, I climbed in behind them.

"Ma'am, you're going to have to get back out. We need room to work, so you can't ride with us."

As I stepped out, I saw Landen open his eyes briefly. I felt like he was telling me he was okay. But just as quickly, his eyes fell shut, and the ambulance doors closed between us.

> "Behold, I give you the authority to trample on serpents and scorpions, and over all the power of the enemy, and nothing shall by any means hurt you."
>
> — LUKE 10:19, NKJV

> "Whoever dwells in the shelter of the Most High will rest in the shadow of the Almighty. I will say of the LORD, "He is my refuge and my fortress, my God, in whom I trust."
>
> — PSALMS 91:1-2 NIV

God, thank You that nothing shall by any means harm us. I rest in Your shelter. I hide in Your shadow. You are my Refuge and Protector. You are my God, and I trust You.

Chapter 5

Breakthroughs in the Chaos

As the ambulance raced away, my heart pounded with a mix of anxiety and determination. There was only one thing on my mind: getting to Landen as quickly as possible. *I need to be by his side right now!* I thought desperately.

Amidst the chaos, a compassionate police officer approached me and calmly informed me that I would ride with him. I followed the officer to his car. He opened the back door and closed it behind me as I anxiously settled.

We immediately left out of the parking lot, trailing the ambulance.

A female officer sat in front, operating a computer. It felt strange sitting there—confined within those four walls that resembled more of a prison than a safe place.

"Ma'am, I need to ask you some questions about the incident," the female officer said.

As her questions went on, my impatience grew stronger. I couldn't help but pound on the glass divider between us and urge them to hurry.

I answered their questions quickly but couldn't help feeling annoyed at their slow pace. *You can ask me this later*, I thought bitterly.

"We need to hurry," I insisted. "I need to see my baby."

"I understand, but we need accurate information for our records."

After a few more questions, the car lapsed into silence, and my tension grew as we sat in the stop-and-go traffic with the lights on and siren blaring. It allowed me glimpses of people in neighboring cars who were oblivious to what was happening inside our chaotic vehicle.

Frustrated by delays, I couldn't bear wasting more time confined within those walls of uncertainty. I started desperately reaching out to Dave and family members to tell them what had happened.

My mom answered, but all I could say was, "Get to Children's. Someone just threw Landen." She couldn't comprehend what I was telling her, and my patience wore thin. I yelled into the phone, "Go to Children's Minneapolis! I'm on my way there with Landen in an ambulance." I hung up.

During the rest of this tumultuous journey to get back to Landen, the rest of my calls went unanswered, leaving me disappointed and angry.

At that moment, something shifted within me. I realized my loved ones would have to find another way to get information if they didn't answer now. I would make no more calls once we arrived at the hospital, because I would be completely focused on fighting for Landen.

With our cop car trailing closely behind the ambulance, my thoughts turned to God. I began praying fervently for His intervention and protection over Landen. "Take the devil's hand off of my baby in Jesus' name," I pleaded, before declaring, "I am a child of God, and no one will take Landen from me. God is the final decision-maker over life and death. I refuse to let fear consume me; this battle belongs to Him alone."

Finally arriving at Children's Hospital in Minneapolis, a team of surgeons stood ready to assess Landen's injuries. Later on, Erika, a PICU nurse, told me that this trauma team is never there all together waiting when a patient arrives. Normally, they would be called in for a situation like this and would arrive as quickly as they could. I was experiencing another miracle that day because they were all there ready to go at the exact moment that Landen desperately needed them.

Every moment mattered; timing was everything. The paramedics had already begun cataloging his extensive wounds—shattered wrists, hands, and elbows; a broken femur; fractured facial bones; and a brain injury.

As I trailed Landen's stretcher through the hospital corridors and into the operating room, I whispered, "He is alive! Bones can heal! God can and will completely restore his body from head to toe."

Inside that lifesaving operating room with the medical drama unfolding before my eyes, I found myself searching for solace through prayer—no fancy words, just a mother's heartfelt plea, "God, use the doctors' hands to heal Landen." I kept at it, praying for his body to be restored entirely, ideally, the way God had given him to me five years before.

The scene was chaotic, but there was a sense of peace in my heart. As the noise in the room rose, someone laid down the law. "Only people who need to talk can speak!" they declared, trying to bring some order to the hectic scene.

A doctor yelled out urgently, "What is his blood pressure?"

Channeling my inner hockey mom spirit and fueled by unwavering faith, I boldly proclaimed from atop my chair, "Perfect!" Sitting didn't seem possible anymore. Even though Landen's external appearance suggested otherwise, I saw beyond the surface and confidently declared his body perfect. That steadfast declaration gave me a profound understanding that Landen would eventually be restored to an ideal state through God's miracle-working power.

As surgeons worked to set Landen's bones and remove his spleen, my prayers became an unwavering soundtrack in that hospital room. There was a lot of hustle and bustle as they prepared him for an MRI. Amidst it all Landen's life hung in a delicate dance between medical expertise and divine intervention. Finally, Landen was ready to move to the MRI room.

The doors swung open, and there they were—my parents and my brother Matt. Our eyes locked, heavy with tears that no words could express. We fell into each other's arms, our sobs mingling as we sank to the ground together. In that brief moment of shared grief, we found a quiet comfort amidst the turmoil—a peace that surpassed understanding.

The MRI was over quickly. When Landen emerged, they were ready to whisk him away again for surgery. "Wait!" I cried out instinctively. "I need to give him a kiss."

A doctor called out firmly yet kindly, "Stop for Mom's kiss—it's important." The bustle ceased; everyone understood the gravity of this simple act of love.

I kissed Landen's face maybe ten times—I lost count in those precious seconds. Looking at his peaceful little face, I felt a surge of hope. God's peace readied my heart for the spiritual fight we were about to face.

"Nana kisses, too," my mom said softly. She stepped forward and gently kissed his forehead with all the tenderness in her heart. Her composure trembled at seeing him so vulnerable. It was an image no one should ever have to witness: their little grandbaby broken but still clinging fiercely to life. Yet an inexplicable peace washed over us all in this hallway which had been lined with uncertainty and fear. We felt profound gratitude because Landen was still with us.

After whispering my goodbyes and watching them take Landen up for surgery, I stood still for a moment—alone but not lonely, because I knew he was surrounded by skilled hands that would be guided by Someone greater than us all.

As they wheeled Landen away, I felt a deep conviction. I knew holding onto any unforgiveness in my heart would hinder God's ability to work through me and answer my prayers.

With an unwavering voice, I yelled out for all to hear, "I forgive the man who did this to Landen!"

My forgiveness was not an act of condoning his actions or wanting him to escape justice. It was a conscious decision to remove him from occupying any more of my thoughts. He wasn't worth it—I no longer allowed him to consume my mind.

Extending forgiveness created room for God's grace and power to flow through me and granted me peace. I no longer needed to worry about this man or seek vengeance because, ultimately, it was God's role

—not mine—to judge him. I laid this burden at God's feet and left it there. I believe my forgiveness of this man was a key development—a breakthrough moment—in the fight for Landen.

From that moment forward, I made a firm commitment: I would no longer dwell on thoughts of this man. My focus shifted entirely toward supporting Landen's recovery and allowing God's healing presence into our lives.

With every fiber of my being, I confidently trusted those doctors' hands while clinging to God's peace—the kind that doesn't require understanding but envelops you completely when you need it most. It was all I had, and I fought to keep my mind on healing without any distractions getting in the way.

Dave wasn't at the hospital yet. It was just me, my parents, and my brother. We remained there together—determined and united—ready to cross every hurdle until Landen was whole again. Despite everything, we knew deep down that he could be flawlessly pieced back together. Landen had already shown us what it meant to fight with everything you've got.

However, we would need everyone for the fight. Dave's arrival at the hospital would prove to be paramount.

> And when they had come to the place called Calvary, there they crucified Him, and the criminals, one on the right hand and the other on the left. Then Jesus said, "Father, forgive them, for they do not know what they do."
>
> — LUKE 23:33-34 NKJV

God, let us be like Jesus, forgiving those who have wronged us.

CHAPTER 6

THE STRENGTH OF A DAD

MY HEART PLUMMETED AT THE SIGHT OF DAVE.

Arriving to the trauma center accompanied by a Sheriff's deputy, Dave looked utterly devastated, the opposite of frantic—more like he was nauseous with distress. He wore black athletic pants and a matching sports jacket—the uniform that took me back to the hockey rink where we'd spent countless hours rooting for our boys.

Dave's eyes met mine in a room swarming with people, and he uttered desperately, "I need my wife." A nurse chimed in to tell us there was a conference room down the hall where we could talk privately.

We made our way into the small room and shut ourselves in. The pain etched in his eyes was palpable and his voice quivered uncontrollably as he said, "I need to know what happened."

Taking a deep breath, I recounted every detail of the ordeal. I started with how we stood on that rock outside the restaurant, waiting for the kids store to open. My voice shook as I relived those horrifying moments—how a man approached us and whispered something to the boys. The whole situation was so incomprehensible and surreal.

The horror of those moments replayed vividly as I continued, "Out of nowhere—without warning or hesitation—he lifted Landen . . . and within mere seconds . . . he ran and hurled him over the edge." Tears welled up in my eyes as I struggled to convey the sheer terror of that act.

No longer able to rein in my emotions, I stood up on chairs right there in that conference room—my arms flailing—to demonstrate how Landen had been thrown over; it felt crucial for Dave to grasp even an ounce of that terror.

As I reenacted that tragic scene before Dave's eyes, it felt like time stood still—this was the frozen moment when our world shattered.

"Who? Who did this?" Dave's urgent inquiry broke through my narrative haze.

My response weighed heavily on our hearts. "I don't know . . . some man who picked him up and ran. All I could do then was bolt down the escalators, screaming, 'Someone threw my baby!' It felt like seconds before I reached Landen—I scooped him up only to hear a woman urging me to put him down gently until help arrived."

Dave knew justice needed to be served, but not by our hands.

Clarity emerged between us as we stood firm in that cramped space. I told Dave, "All I care about right now is ensuring Landen keeps fighting for his life." Everything else fell secondary—including justice, which would be left for others outside these walls.

Our conversation may have been brief, but it resonated deeply. We left the room understanding implicitly that we had distinct roles during this crisis, but also that we were united toward the same end goal. Our job was to navigate through this ordeal together as parents, shouldering whatever came next without distraction. Haden and Haley still needed their dad around while their brother fought valiantly upstairs. I would not leave Landen's side.

Dave shielded me from further questioning or stress by handling communications himself—he engaged Bloomington police downstairs, ensuring they didn't approach me directly. His protective instincts meant all my focus could remain on being present beside Landen once he came out of surgery. I was thankful for my husband.

Landen's well-being consumed every thought—the whereabouts or fate of the man who threw him never crossed my mind after I released him to God. Somehow, God had enabled forgiveness to flow freely out of my heartache, allowing His judgment to be executed rather than my own.

During this ordeal, I came to greatly appreciate my upbringing in the church. It was interesting that these truths lay deep inside me, revealed at a time of desperate need. Growing up, I had always been strong in my faith, and I loved God deeply. But it wasn't until my world shattered and desperation set in to save Landen that the depth of those truths emerged from within me.

In those desperate moments, something unexpected happened—I found a boldness that surprised me. I thought back on how I yelled at those around me in the mall to pray for Landen, how I boldly prayed aloud over his broken body. That meek young teacher who didn't want to pray aloud during school assemblies now felt like a shadow of who I was becoming. It felt like the Holy Spirit was speaking through me, giving me strength and guiding my words. God was endowing me with His mighty power to fight a spiritual battle against the enemy for Landen's life and recovery.

I understood how much I relied on God's guidance and how He had equipped me with what I needed to face this unimaginable challenge. It was like I had been preparing for this moment my entire life. Everything around me faded except the focal point of ensuring Landen's healing and recovery—a need only God could meet. But He chooses to work through the prayers and faith of His people.

I said over and over, "Landen, you've got this!"

The journey ahead would test our resilience and faith. It would require incredible teamwork and cohesion between the work of medical professionals and faith—our family's faith in the God of miracles. The hospital room echoed with anticipation as we witnessed what could only be described as Minnesota's true miracle unfolding before our eyes.

"With His love, He will calm all your fears."

Kari Hoffmann

— Zephaniah 3:17 NLT

Lord, cast out fear and give us supernatural faith in our time of desperate need.

Chapter 7

What Just Happened?

To spare us the chaos of the waiting room, a hospital employee named Doug found us an expansive conference room on the PICU floor where we could all gather to wait for Landen. It was a sanctuary, and I was so thankful for Doug, who acted as a bridge between me and the doctors.

After the intimate moments downstairs with my immediate family, I entered the conference room to a different scene. The noise and the presence of extended relatives surprised me, and I felt an overwhelming sense of unconditional love and support. Their presence and their determined faith reassured me that we could handle whatever lay ahead for Landen.

Amidst the growing crowd in the conference room, one person stood out: Betsy. Her presence was an anchor for me, grounding us in the reality of what we had just witnessed. I was relieved to see her there, knowing she had raced to the hospital alone, driven by adrenaline-fueled fear and uncertainty.

I pulled Betsy from the crowd and took her to a different floor in search of privacy. As we stood by a coffee machine, I asked for her thoughts on what happened.

"As soon as I saw him go over the edge, I screamed," she said, wrapping trembling hands around her coffee cup. "I grabbed for Will and held him close to me, and I watched the man scramble to his feet and run away. I was so scared, but I also felt this incredibly strong conviction. I told myself he is not going to get away! I watched him closely and tried to memorize as much as I could about him so I could tell the police.

"In all the chaos, we must have both thrown our purses, and I just stood there in shock with Will beside me. Then, a woman came out of nowhere and told me to go. She said she would take care of Will. It's the craziest thing, but I knew I could trust her, so I went after you."

I thought of how profound that was. A stranger had just committed a horribly unspeakable act on one child right in front of Betsy, yet she could trust a different stranger to take care of her child. This assured me that most of the people around us are good. It's amazing that when a tragedy takes place, we can count on our fellow man to step in and help. As bad as the world may seem, there is still so much good in it if we look around and take notice.

I nodded for her to go on.

"When I found you, you were struggling to breathe and asking for water. I started asking people at the food places if I could get some water, but everyone refused. That made me so mad! Then, this kind-looking woman saw me panicking and gave me a bottle of water. That really restored my faith in people. But everything was happening so fast that I never got to give you the water. I was still holding the water when a police officer walked up and asked for my help to identify the man who did this.

"They interviewed me about details of everything while we walked toward a police car where the man was sitting—as if he had no cares in the world! He would've gotten away, except that there was another man who saw him running and knocked him on the ground."

Upon hearing this, I wanted to tell the heroic stranger, "Thank you for following your gut and helping us capture him! You are our angel. We will never forget you."

"When I saw him sitting there in the police car, I immediately told the police, 'That's the man! Sitting right there in the police car—that's the one who threw Landen over the balcony!' I wanted to throw that glass water bottle at him!" She finished, her voice rising in anger.

I couldn't help but imagine what might have transpired if Dave had been there instead. He was a fiercely protective dad. Who knows what he might have done out of sheer compulsion? It was a relief that Betsy—not Dave—had to identify the man.

Seeing him in that cop car—safe and alive while Landen was fighting for his life—must have been an incredibly infuriating sight. Such a despicable act would stir up emotions that would be overwhelming for any parent.

I listened in shock as Betsy continued her account. "After I identified the attacker, I went back to get Will. The lady who was watching him had our purses too. Then I found you when they were getting Landen loaded onto the stretcher. You were urgently telling me to find your phone and call Dave, but I didn't know the code to unlock it. I called Tony, and thankfully, he found Dave's number in the football directory and called him for me. I'm so glad I followed you so I could give you your phone before you left."

I remembered her appearing out of nowhere with my phone in hand—a moment when our connection felt genuinely divine. As we recalled all of these details standing beside the coffee maker, we talked a million miles a minute, trying to remember everything.

Betsy's strength and determination as she made her way to the hospital after witnessing the unthinkable astounded me. It could have easily been her son who suffered instead of Landen—best friends torn apart by a cruel hand. The weight of that realization made us both sick to our stomachs.

Reliving those moments with Betsy was both heart-racing and comforting as we tried to understand what had transpired. Through tears, laughter, and hugs, we realized that we both needed new clothes due to not caring about finding a bathroom during this ordeal—a shared vulnerability that only strengthened our bond and also made us laugh for a quick minute.

What in the world just happened? I thought as we returned to the conference room.

Before I rejoined the group, I stopped for a moment to think. In that one terrifying moment, our lives changed forever. It was a nightmare no mother should ever have to endure—the sudden threat that our child's life could be snatched away in an instant.

I knew Landen was fighting with every ounce of his being to hold onto life. I shouted these assurances so Landen could hear me, "Not today, Devil! Landen is going to live and not die! Take your hands off of him, Satan!"

Landen heard me; I'm sure of it. His sheer determination and willpower became a beacon of hope for all of us. Landen's fight for survival reminded me that miracles can happen in our darkest moments. His resilience was a powerful lesson. It was a reminder not to take life for granted—that life is something to fight for.

So let us cherish each day with our children, holding them close and treasuring every precious moment together. Life is fragile and unpredictable; it can change in an instant. Let us be grateful for life's simple blessings—the gift of waking up each morning and breathing is beautiful.

Landen faced unimaginable challenges, but his fight reminds us that miracles are possible when we refuse to give up hope.

Dave immediately noticed me as I returned to the conference room. Crowded spaces were not his forte, and he didn't find a sense of peace in being surrounded by family the way I did. Plus, Dave never sits; he's a pacer. He grabbed my hand tightly, pulling me away from the crowd so we could walk the hallways together.

As we walked, we took turns praying out loud and held tightly to each other's hands.

"Lord, don't let evil prevail over Landen's life. Let your healing touch be upon him."

"God, place your hand of protection over Landen, and please let us have him back."

"Lord, guide the doctors' hands to bring healing and recovery to our little boy."

As we reentered the conference room, I saw more people had shown up to support us. Despite the overwhelming situation, a deep sense of peace settled within me. I knew Landen was stable and would ultimately be okay. Even as tears filled the eyes of every person who came, I reassured them with confidence that Landen would overcome this trial. I felt it in my heart, and I was standing on that truth!

Courtney, my beloved cousin and neighbor, entered the room in tears. She looked frantic and completely devastated. We shared such a strong bond that when she cries, I cry, too. When she laughs, I laugh alongside her. She had been trying to reach me on my phone all day.

Earlier, I had given my phone to my sister Mandy and asked her to answer my calls. When Courtney called, I requested that she go to my house and pack some clothes and toiletries so that I would have the essentials at the hospital. I knew it would be a long time before I left.

The sight of Courtney arriving with my clothes bag in hand while trembling with devastation will forever be etched in my memory—a stark reminder of how fragile life can be and how important it is to lean on one another during times of crisis.

Because so many people were starting to show up, Doug, the hospital coordinator, implemented a security measure. He asked me to provide a code word for trusted individuals to gain access. I entrusted the task to my family. They devised a secret word and shared it with those who were still on the way, allowing them to enter without being questioned.

This extra security didn't seem particularly significant at the time, but I later realized this was a way for God to give the situation a greater measure of peace and safety. It was a reminder that He was in control and orchestrating every aspect of this story, assuring us that His presence would guide us throughout our journey and keep us safe every step of the way.

I felt restless as I waited with my family in the conference room for Landen's initial surgery to be over. Impatience grew within me as I anxiously awaited the arrival of a doctor who would provide a report on his condition.

Betsy could sense my unease, and unexpectedly, she reached out to offer her support by handing me a rosary she kept in her car—a symbol of faith and strength. It was a gesture that touched my heart deeply. She said, "I don't usually carry this with me, but I had it in my car today. I think maybe you needed it."

As someone who did not grow up Catholic, I wasn't sure what to do with the rosary. However, I recognized its significance as a cross. Gratefully, I accepted Betsy's kind gesture and placed the rosary in my back pocket.

This small act of kindness reminded me that the love and support we have from those around us is invaluable during challenging times. The support and prayers of everyone in the room gave me peace and assurance, calming my impatience and anxiety.

Finally, a doctor entered the room.

"And we know that in all things God works for the good of those who love him, who have been called according to his purpose".

— ROMANS 8:28, NIV

"Above all else, guard your heart, for everything you do flows from it."

— PROVERBS 4:23 NIV

Lord, thank You for Your promise to bring good even from the storms that devastate our lives. Help us to be careful what we think about, and guard our hearts during times of trial.

Chapter 8

The Prognosis

The atmosphere was tense with anticipation, and we were all filled with adrenaline, relief, and hope. We'd spent the entire day holding onto each other, shedding tears, and offering prayers—all while waiting for this one moment to arrive.

It was time for the four doctors to come together as a team and share their findings about Landen's condition and his prognosis for recovery. I hadn't had a chance to think about anything other than survival. But now, as we braced ourselves, I took a deep breath and prepared for what lay ahead. I was ready.

The first to speak was Dr. Halverson, the neurologist. Although he brought us what was good news considering the circumstances, he remained cautious in his delivery. Perhaps he was trying not to give us false hope, knowing things could change quickly. "The initial CT scan shows multiple facial fractures and some brain injury, but, incredibly, it looks very good overall."

He continued, "Landen's primary injury was to the front of his head—and this part is going to sound much worse than it probably is—but it caused a very small part of his brain to die. Unfortunately, that part of the brain can't grow back. This may affect personality. It could make him more impulsive, but it will not affect his overall motor function.

"Right now, Landen is intubated and he's in a medically-induced coma. The coma is necessary for pain and inflammation control. We'll keep him intubated until the inflammation has come down and he starts showing signs of wanting to wake up."

When Dr. Halverson spoke, his face displayed deep concern and empathy shone through his eyes. I could see his genuine care and compassion for Landen's well-being. I knew we were in good hands, surrounded by a team of doctors who truly cared about Landen's recovery. *Thank You, God!*

My sister Mandy interrupted with an anxious question, "Will Landen be able to lead a normal everyday life?"

Dr. Halverson, squinting slightly and nodding cautiously, answered, "Yes, he will, but it will take time. Like I said, the injury to his frontal lobe could cause personality changes and increased impulsivity. We sometimes have to purposely remove small parts of the frontal lobe from people with cancer, and they are able to live a normal life afterward, so this is not something where we're not sure what is going to happen.

"We will need a repeat CT scan at midnight tonight to be completely sure of the extent of his injuries. However, we are confident that Landen *will* walk, talk, and be himself again."

The room fell into silent joy. We were overwhelmed by gratitude and a collective sense of relief. We couldn't help but utter prayers of gratitude, and a tearful "Praise the Lord!" escaped my lips. This was one step closer to overcoming the hurdles we faced. I knew, without a doubt, that I'd be getting my baby back! This was nothing short of a miracle, and we were ready to hear what the rest of the team had to say.

We'd reached a crucial turning point, our worst fears had eased as the doctors illuminated a path to recovery. The journey ahead would not be easy, but with Landen's strength and resilience, and these remarkable doctors' expertise, we believed that he would triumph.

Holding our breaths, we eagerly awaited the next doctor's information that would shape Landen's journey toward healing.

Dr. Curtis, the ENT surgeon, delivered the news. "Landen has fractures in various parts of his face, including the upper jaw on both sides, the back part of the left upper jaw, the floor and roof of the eye sockets, and the middle area of the eye sockets on both sides. He also has extensive fractures in the sinuses between the eyes and in the front and back parts of the skull. Lastly, there are fractures near the ears and a complex palate fracture. Yes, I know this sounds severe, but all these injuries can be repaired, and Landen's face will fully heal over time. The ENT team will be here to provide continual support and make sure that Landen makes a full recovery."

A surge of relief washed over me as Dr. Curtis spoke. I was immensely grateful, and his competence and compassion humbled me.

Next was Dr. Engels, the orthopedic doctor. As he presented his report, showing tremendous concern and emotion, I knew he genuinely wanted to help my little boy. "Landen has fractures in multiple areas of his body. The right leg has a broken thigh bone, and the right elbow suffered numerous fractures, accompanied by an open wound. On the left side, there is a forearm fracture with a small wound and a severely broken elbow. Thankfully, there are no fractures in Landen's left leg. Lastly, there are wounds on his left index and middle fingers."

Jared, my brother-in-law, interrupted with a puzzled inquiry, "So, after Landen was thrown off a balcony, all we're talking about is bones?" I could see the wonder in his eyes as he searched for reassurance.

Without hesitation, a bold response escaped my lips, "You bet! Bones can heal! Bones can heal!" It was a moment of profound clarity, a testament to our unshakable belief that Landen would heal completely. I did not doubt that God's hand was on our situation.

Dr. Engels echoed my words, optimistically saying, "Yes, it appears that way at this point."

Overwhelmed with peace and confidence, my heart brimmed with anticipation. I was ready to see Landen, to be by his side, and to move forward, knowing without a shadow of a doubt that he would heal completely, just as we had believed throughout this entire day of miracles.

Also in the room with us was Dr. Wahoff, the PICU surgeon who led the remarkable team of medical professionals working tirelessly to save Landen. Upon Landen's arrival, Dr. Wahoff had swiftly removed Landen's spleen in an emergency procedure. He explained to us that, out of all the organs in the body, the spleen was the one that needed to be addressed urgently to prevent further bleeding.

It was bittersweet to learn Landen could live perfectly fine without his spleen. Removing it had saved his life. *Thank You, God.*

As the team informed me that Landen would soon be brought to a room, my heart swelled excitedly. Family members, including Dave, started to say their goodbyes.

"Kari, I just can't bear to see him like this right now," Dave said, his voice shaking. "I'm going to go home to be with the twins and make sure they're handling everything okay. Your mom said she'd stay and look after you and Landen tonight."

"Of course," I said, pulling Dave into a lingering hug. I trusted him to watch over our twins so I could be with Landen.

Everyone slowly exited until it was just me and my parents left in the room. Finally, the doctors said we could go see Landen.

We quickly made our way down the hallway, eager to reach Landen's room. Every step filled me with a mixture of emotions, but above all, an overwhelming feeling of unconditional love drove me forward. I couldn't wait to shower Landen with kisses, letting him know I was there for him, filled with unwavering love and determination.

Landen, I'm here . . .

"Then Jesus said, 'Come to me, all of you who are weary and carry heavy burdens, and I will give you rest.'"

— MATTHEW 11:28 NLT

Thank You, Lord, for carrying our burdens and giving us rest, even in life's most troublesome times.

Chapter 9

Finding Rest

Entering Landen's room, I saw that he was bandaged from head to foot, with drain tubes siphoning off fluid from his stomach and spine. A maze of wires came out from his body, and monitors surrounded his bed, reporting every aspect of his condition.

I immediately went to the bed and held his hand, standing in awe. I couldn't resist kissing his cheeks, longing to take away any pain he might be feeling.

> "Peace I leave with you; my peace I give you. I do not give to you as the world gives. Do not let your hearts be troubled and do not be afraid."

But he seemed peaceful, secure in his hospital bed. He was safe, and no one could harm him. A sense of calm washed over me, and I felt profoundly grateful to be by his side.

My mom approached his bed tearfully, bending down to place gentle kisses on him, while my dad stood nearby, his lips moving in prayer.

We stayed this way for a while, each of us taking in that fact that Landen was alive and safe with us.

As the clock neared midnight, my parents prepared to leave because Lindsay, my best friend since childhood, was on the way. My mom bustled about making a bed for me and putting my clothes away, while I met with nurses as they came in and out.

Giving Landen a final kiss, my mom turned to me for a hug, saying, "Lindsay should be here any minute. We'll be back right at

8:00 am with coffee. I love you, sweetheart."

"Thank you, Mom. I love you, too," I said, returning her hug.

After giving Dad a hug and kiss as well, they left, and it was just Landen, me, and the beeping of life-support machines in his room.

The night nurse, Katrin, entered the room and introduced herself. She informed me that it was time for Landen's second MRI, and to my relief, I was allowed to accompany him. The thought of not leaving his side brought me comfort.

We began our journey to the MRI room. Many nurses gathered to assist with Landen's bed, along with all of the necessary equipment, through the hallways. I followed closely behind, trying to reach Landen's side and hold his hand, but sometimes having to fall back toward the end of his bed due to the congestion in the corridors.

As we reached the basement where the MRI room was located, I caught sight of Lindsay. I had never been so overjoyed to see her. I knew I wouldn't be alone during the day's final test.

We embraced tightly and began talking rapidly, our words overlapping. We laughed, and I said, "You first."

"I was nursing the baby on the couch when a news story came on talking about a child being thrown off the balcony at the mall. I knew you were going today, so I tried to call you over and over and tell you not to go, but you didn't answer. I finally got in touch with your sister, and she told me what happened. I couldn't believe it!" she said, her voice breaking as she pulled me in for another hug.

"I'm sorry I didn't call you back. I didn't mean to leave you with nothing to do but worry," I responded as we drew apart.

"It's okay," she replied, wiping away fresh tears. "I'm just glad I can be here now."

We had actually invited Lindsay to go with us, but she declined, not wanting to expose her newborn to the extreme cold. I can only imagine the "what ifs" that must have run through her mind that day.

Lindsay and I sat together and waited for Landen to complete his test, filling the silence and finding comfort in each other's presence.

When Landen emerged, Dr. Halverson was walking alongside his bed. He said, "His scans show no change, which is good news. That means his condition is stable. So you all can return to your room for the rest of the night."

I felt immense relief and was grateful to have Lindsay there to share this moment of joy.

Back in his room, I changed into pajamas, and we tucked Landen in for the night. I made sure his beloved blankie was tucked under his head and within his grasp. I gave him a final kiss and whispered assurances of his safety and my love for him.

When it was time for Lindsay to head home, we embraced again.

"Thank you for coming," I told her.

"Of course. I'm always here for you. I'll be back in the morning to check on both of you." She said goodnight and then let herself out.

I checked on Landen again before settling down on the couch. I fell asleep to the beeping machines, finding solace in their rhythm, knowing the beeps meant that Landen was still with us. As I drifted off, I felt God had cradled me in His arms, granting me peace and serenity.

Good night, my sweet baby.

"But I will restore you to health and heal your wounds,' declares the LORD."

— JEREMIAH 30:17 NIV

"In peace I will lie down and sleep, for you alone, O LORD, will keep me safe."

— PSALM 4:8 NLT

Thank You, Lord, for promising to restore us to health and heal our wounds. Thank You that we can lie down and sleep in peace, for You alone will keep us safe.

Chapter 10

Staying Focused amid Book and TV Offers, and International News Coverage

The next morning, I hurriedly got dressed and brushed my teeth. We were in an intensive around-the-clock care room, enclosed by glass doors, with doctors and nurses bustling about. These rooms, reserved for patients needing constant care, were nicknamed "the fishbowl rooms" due to their complete lack of privacy. The nurses started talking to me once I looked presentable, wearing comfortable clothes and my hair in a bun.

Katrin briefed Paige, our day nurse, on Landen's condition before turning to me. "I think you should start writing everything down in a journal. That will help keep your mind and hands busy. If you need anything, even to talk, we are all here for you and Landen."

"I think that's a great idea. I really appreciate everything you did to look after Landen through the night," I responded.

"I was happy to help your sweet little boy," she said with a smile and waved goodbye.

I had just settled down beside Landen when Dave and his mom arrived. I went down to the lobby to meet them because Dave didn't feel ready to see Landen yet. He handed me a bag filled with items that Haden and Haley packed for Landen. They didn't know the extent of what had happened to him. All they knew was that he was at the mall with me, had fallen off the balcony, and was now in the hospital recovering. I had yet to speak to them. Dave told them I had to be with Landen for now, but I could talk to them on the phone after school.

The bag contained some toys: Landen's puppy stuffed animal, a Goofy plush that Landen loved, and a Minecraft journal Landen had gotten from the school book fair.

When I saw the Minecraft journal, covered in Landen's scribbles, I thought it was the perfect place to start my writing. It would be my journal, which already held his scribbles and memories. I decided to document the daily whirlwind while processing my thoughts and emotions. Even though understanding why this happened—or what kind of challenges we still had to face— seemed impossible, I resolved that I would record Landen's progress alongside my hopes, anger, frustration, and unwavering trust in God.

After I returned to Landen's room, I began to write. With giant letters filling the first page, I wrote, "Day Zero: The Day the Angels Saved You!"

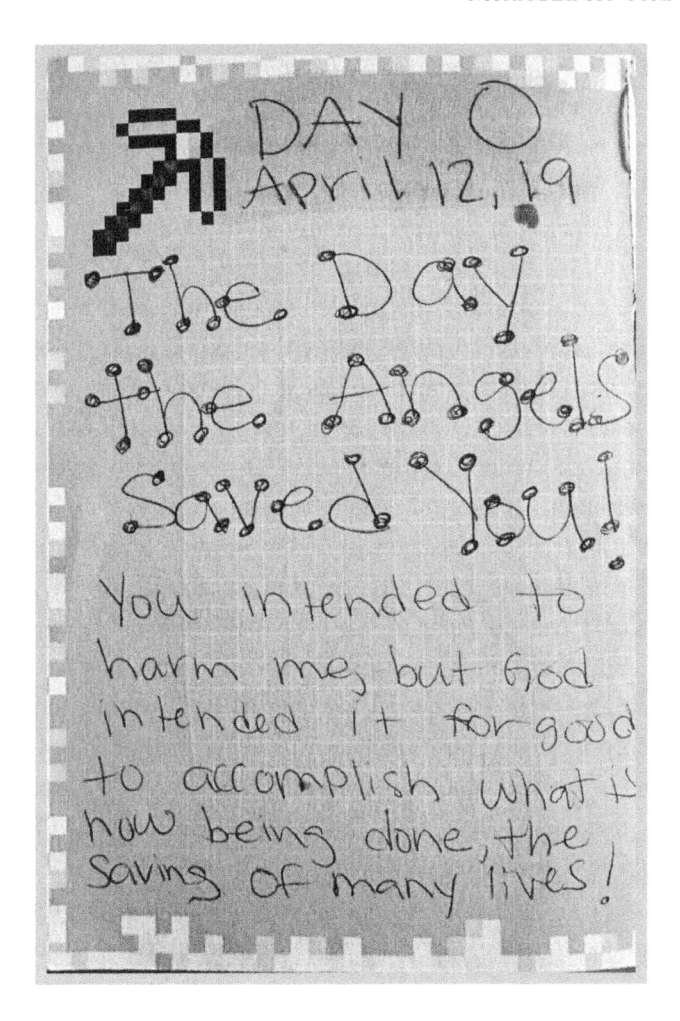

> DAY 0
> April 12, 19
> The Day the Angels Saved You!
> You intended to harm me, but God intended it for good to accomplish what is now being done, the saving of many lives!

At the time, we drew hope and comfort from Psalm 91:11-12 (NIV), "For he will command his angels concerning you to guard you in all your ways; they will lift you up in their hands, so that you will not strike your foot against a stone."

I began my journal entry for Day One with the bold heading "Recovery," holding onto the hope that every day would be one step closer to Landen's healing. Throughout the day and into the night, I recorded each step of progress. Because I couldn't communicate with Landen in his comatose state, journaling gave me a way to speak to and reassure him.

The IV is getting removed from your stomach because it is no longer necessary!

Got all new bandages, and the bleeding has stopped! No more bleeding!

The IV came out of your leg last night! We're removing one thing at a time.

Despite the seriousness of Landen's condition, I considered every moment a cause for celebration, and I thanked God for these positive developments. I was seeing progress unfold before my eyes, and it filled me with wonder and hope. Everything was falling into place one step at a time and with incredible speed. The doctors marveled at how his body was knitting itself back together so perfectly.

In faith, I wrote a message to Landen in my journal, proclaiming, "Landen, everything is PERFECT." I told every doctor who visited us that day that I wanted them to use the word "PERFECT" to describe Landen's condition, coming alongside me in optimism and faith.

Amazingly, they understood the significance of my request and began incorporating it into their reports. They would candidly discuss the obstacles we still had to overcome but conclude their reports by affirming that, aside from those challenges, Landen was PERFECT. Hearing those words from the doctors made me smile, and I earnestly thanked them for their positive assessments. It gave me profound hope and assurance for the days ahead, strengthening my resolve as I proclaimed in faith that God would bring full healing to Landen's body.

As I continued to write, my words overflowed with love and encouragement for Landen. I wanted him to know how well he was doing and how much I believed in his body's healing power.

I reminded him of the remarkable way he had survived the fall and how resilient he had been, with angels surrounding him every step of the way.

With a tender touch, I acknowledged the wound on his head, recognizing that it would be a scar on his face—a constant reminder of what he went through. At first, I felt an ache in my heart, knowing that the scar would be visible for all to see, forever etched in his features.

But as I reflected, my perspective shifted. I embraced the realization that this scar, rather than a mark of hurt, would be a symbol of the miraculous healing God bestowed upon Landen. It would show the world that miracles happen and serve as a testament to what God accomplished, overpowering the harm that man inflicted.

I wanted Landen to understand that God's healing power encompassed every inch of his body, from the crown of his head to the tips of his toes. I expressed my profound gratitude for being blessed with the greatest gift in Landen, who I believed carried a divine purpose to spread joy, God's love, and a reminder that miracles still exist. I assured him that my love would never waver, and I pledged to remain by his side through it all.

But the peace I found in the Lord as I sat in Landen's hospital room was a calm in the eye of the hurricane of our life. To navigate the overwhelming challenges of this journey, Dave and I knew we needed a well-defined plan with clear roles. Our main objective was to keep this story as private as possible, allowing us to heal in peace while also shielding Haden and Haley, who were only seven years old, from the harsh reality of what had transpired. However, despite our intentions, the news of Landen's ordeal had already become a national and international news story.

I believe our story garnered such widespread attention because it resonated vividly with every mother's terror. A joyful trip to the mall turned into a living nightmare, with a child torn away right before our eyes, facing an attempted murder. The sheer horror of the situation struck a chord with mothers everywhere who could imagine themselves in my shoes. It became a story that evoked deep empathy and understanding from anyone who could place themselves, even for a moment, in our unimaginable experience.

The press constantly hounded us, knocking on our door at home and circling our cul-de-sac in search of photos of Haden, Haley, and Dave. Our phones rang incessantly, with people offering television, book, and magazine deals if we would share our story. To handle these external pressures, Dave was responsible for dealing with the near constant requests from the press, addressing the media when appropriate, taking care of Haden and Haley, and managing additional demands from our day-to-day life that still had to be handled.

Meanwhile, I deliberately protected my focus and stayed unwaveringly dedicated to Landen's healing journey. I only answered my phone if I recognized the caller, and I consciously avoided checking emails, Facebook messages, or instant messages. I asked my mom or Dave to inform me in person if there was any critical information that someone felt was necessary for me to know. Otherwise, I kindly requested not to be told, as I wished to remain unaware and protected from the noise and negativity of the outside world.

As we began this new chapter in our lives, Dave took on the crucial responsibility of running the household and shielding Haden and Haley from the pain and terror surrounding the situation. His main goals were to preserve a sense of normalcy for the kids and to be present for our family during this difficult time. Thankfully, Dave's workplace, Love's Travel Stops, played a remarkable role in supporting our family. They granted him as much time off as needed and even provided Dave with a personal driver each day while Landen was recovering.

This was a major help because it was incredibly difficult for Dave to drive to Minneapolis every day and deal with the stress of traffic and parking while Landen was fighting for his life in the hospital. This simple yet thoughtful gesture lifted a significant burden off Dave, allowing him to focus on supporting Landen without the stress of navigating traffic.

Each morning, the driver would pick him up, and during the ride, Dave—who rarely found time to listen to worship music—would use the quiet time to prepare his heart and mind for the long day ahead. At the hospital, Dave spent hours walking the hallways, speaking with doctors, and seeking reassurance, while I stayed by Landen's bedside.

By 2:00 pm each day, the driver would take him back home so he could pick up the twins from school. This routine became his full-time job during the most critical month of Landen's recovery. Dave's boss even visited the hospital to walk the halls with him, demonstrating the extraordinary kindness and support we never knew we needed during such a painful time. I even was able to utilize the driver a few times myself. It was so nice to have, because driving in downtown Minneapolis is busy—there's nowhere to park and it's very stressful.

With the pressures of work and transportation lifted, Dave could focus on our family and the well-being of our son. To ensure he got crucial updates on Landen's condition, Dave arrived at the hospital at the same time each day and then left in time to pick up Haden and Haley from school. This routine allowed him to establish a balanced rhythm between the twin's needs and Landen's well-being. Although he longed to see his youngest son, Dave had made a personal decision not to visit Landen in his room until he had awakened from his coma. It was an act of love and self-preservation to shield himself from the heart-wrenching sight of Landen's vulnerable state. Instead, Dave communicated with me through texts or would ask a nurse to bring me out if he needed to discuss anything.

In those overwhelming moments when Dave carried the weight of the outside world on his shoulders, my parents played critical roles in supporting me in the hospital. My mom, Kathy, became my lifeline. She understood the importance of having me care for myself, knowing I rarely left Landen's room. She brought me breakfast and coffee each morning and made sure my small fridge was always stocked with snacks and drinks. With her support, I could stay within my protective bubble and focus on my vital role as Landen's mom.

My mom also stayed by Landen's bedside in the mornings, allowing me to slip away for a quick shower and some personal rejuvenation. These moments away from Landen were necessary for my well-being, even though I never wanted to leave his room. We lovingly called this task "kiss duty." My mom would stand near Landen's bed and hold his hand or foot, offering gentle kisses to remind him that he was never alone.

My dad also came to the hospital, joining me for daily walks to get some air and refresh my mind. His unwavering faith, prayers, and protective nature were always there for me. His endearing lack of direction when navigating the winding hallways of the hospital also became lighthearted moments that brought warmth and fun to our journey, giving us a chance to temporarily escape from the weightiness of our reality. After taking these short walks around the hospital, I would return feeling refreshed and ready to face whatever challenges the day had in store for us.

As my world shifted and Landen and I settled into our new home, I found myself making a conscious effort to push away thoughts of the attacker and the harm he inflicted. Instead, I chose to focus my mind on the hopeful signs of healing that were emerging. I treasured every affirmation that God was at work, healing Landen's body day by day.

I chose to release the fear and bitterness that threatened to consume me. With gratitude as my anchor and God as my guide, I was ready to face whatever lay ahead.

"When your faith is tested, you learn to be patient."

— JAMES 1:3 ERV

"Get rid of all bitterness, rage and anger, brawling and slander, along with every form of malice."

— EPHESIANS 4:31 NIV

Lord, help us take our thoughts captive in obedience to You. Empower us to rid ourselves of all bitterness, and fill our hearts with faith as we walk through challenges.

Chapter 11

A Chance at Life

I GOT PREGNANT WITH EACH OF OUR CHILDREN THROUGH IN VITRO fertilization. When we decided to undergo IVF, I knew in my heart that I would give each embryo a chance at life. Many people who do IVF end up with 8-10 embryos. Fortunately, we were only blessed with four, as I don't know what we would have done with ten!

We decided to implant two of the embryos initially and were blessed with Haden and Haley. The bond I felt with my babies was unlike anything I'd ever experienced. It became my biggest desire to care for them, which led me to leave my job as a second-grade teacher. I wanted to be there for every milestone, every little need, and every moment of growth. But it was no walk in the park. Dave and I went into survival mode, barely finding time to eat before rushing off to sleep, hoping for some rest before the cries started again.

But amidst the exhaustion, I learned the value of patience. I remember appreciating the little things and letting go of what I couldn't control. During this time, I came to realize that the challenging moments don't last forever, even if it feels like they will never end.

Dave and I weren't quite ready to welcome another baby when Haden and Haley turned two, but there was an undeniable feeling deep within me that our family wasn't complete yet. We agreed it was time to chase that dream despite the challenges ahead. We met with the doctor, who was adamant about avoiding another set of twins. So, this time around, we chose to implant a single embryo.

The waiting game commenced, and though my excitement was tinged with caution, I couldn't help but remember the joy of bringing a life into the world. We were elated when we received the news of my pregnancy. Sadly, that joy was short-lived, as I experienced a devastating miscarriage a week later. It was an immense heartbreak, but we were determined not to let go of the hope that we still had one more chance to expand our family beyond four.

Though the doctor cautioned us about the slim odds of the last embryo surviving, we decided to press on. The statistics were against us, but we had unwavering faith. We were eager to try again, even if the outcome was uncertain.

As the days dragged by, I couldn't help but feel a mix of anxiety and excitement. Sitting with my mom in a shopping center parking lot, waiting for that life-changing phone call, I sought solace in her presence. I longed for the news, regardless of whether it brought the overwhelming joy of a positive pregnancy or the sorrow of another loss.

When the call finally came, my apprehension became wild joy as I heard the words, "I'm happy to tell you that you are pregnant!" The due date? January—my very own birth month. It was an indescribable moment that left me speechless, shaking and crying tears of pure happiness. The thought that I would get to be a mom to one more little soul felt like an absolute miracle.

In celebration, we purchased a gender-neutral newborn outfit, symbolizing our anticipation for the changes our expanding family would undergo. And oh, what a change it would be. We were ready to welcome this new chapter with open arms, knowing that even amidst the inevitable challenges, our hearts overflowed with love, and the joy of parenthood would make it all worthwhile.

We were ready for Landen.

"I will not cause pain without allowing something new to be born, says the Lord."

— Isaiah 66:9 NCV

Lord, You are always creating something new! Thank You so much that we do not have to stay in the pain of the past, but can always look ahead full of hope for the good future you have for us.

Chapter 12

A Special Place in My Heart

Katie, my cousin from Washington, has always held a special place in my heart. Since the day I was born, she has been by my side, guiding me through life. With a ten-year age gap between us, I looked up to her with admiration and wanted nothing more than to emulate her. Katie frequently babysat my brother, my sister, and me, and those moments were filled with boundless joy.

Over time, Katie got married and moved away due to her husband's military service, but our bond remained unbreakable. I would visit her wherever the military took her, witnessing her journey as a mother. Katie eventually gave birth to twelve beautiful children, and with every visit, I eagerly absorbed all the experiences and wisdom she had to offer. When I discovered I was pregnant with Haley and Haden, my first instinct was to travel to Washington for Katie's guidance, knowing she would be the perfect mentor to help me navigate this new chapter as a mother.

During my visit, Katie showered me with invaluable advice and knowledge, sharing all the nuances of motherhood that only someone with firsthand experience could pass on. I listened intently, filling pages with notes as I soaked in her wisdom. It was an unforgettable experience, and upon returning home, my suitcase overflowed with all the gifts Katie and her children generously prepared for me at my baby shower.

Armed with the belief that I had everything under control, I eagerly awaited the arrival of my babies. However, reality hit hard. Sleep deprivation and the challenges of caring for twins quickly reminded me that being a parent was not as easy as Katie made it appear. I vividly remember the exhaustion that engulfed me as Haley, one of my twins, proved to be a difficult baby who resisted soothing cuddles. It was a humbling experience that shattered any illusions of effortless motherhood.

Katie's influence remained unwavering through all the ups and downs. Her guidance and support have been instrumental in shaping my journey as a mother. Even though I discovered that my path may differ from hers, my admiration for Katie grew stronger. She inspires me to be the best mother I can be, reminding me that even amidst the challenges, the love and dedication we pour into our children will fuel their growth and bring immeasurable love and joy.

Katie rushed to our side as soon as she heard what happened, and her presence became a pivotal source of strength in the first few days after the attack on Landen. I didn't know she was coming, but when I saw her enter Landen's room on the second day after the attack, her presence brought me immense relief.

"I came to pray," was the first thing Katie said. I got up to embrace her and thank her for coming. Then, she stood sentinel beside Landen's bed, holding her Bible and silently offering heartfelt prayers. Katie stayed with us throughout the day and evening, deeply engaged in continuous prayer.

As she prayed, I sat calmly at the foot of Landen's bed, gently touching his hands and feet and placing tender kisses upon him. The room was filled with instrumental worship music, as I believed it would create an atmosphere of joy, laughter, and singing, encouraging Landen to fight. Wrapped securely and connected to various medical devices, I could only see Landen's eyes, toes, and hands. His eyes remained closed in his comatose state, and he relied on a ventilator to breathe. There was also the drain tube to remove excess fluid from around his brain, the feeding tube, a heart monitor, an oxygen monitor, and an IV.

As the night settled and visitors left, Katie remained by Landen's side, her lips continually moving in silent prayer. Around 9:00 pm, she insisted that I get some rest and assured me she would take over kiss duty and receive updates from the nurses. She promised to wake me if there was any important information I needed to know. Thankful for the opportunity to sleep, I took two Benadryl and went to bed, knowing Katie would be there in the morning to continue her prayers for one more day before heading home.

When I woke up at 4:00 am, Katie was no longer there, but I knew she would return later that morning. I gazed at Landen's precious face, noticing that the spinal fluids draining through a tube in his nose were diminishing. It felt like a significant victory, and I confidently declared that, in the mighty name of Jesus, the fluid was gone, checking it off our list of small steps toward complete and perfect healing.

> "And the prayer offered in faith will make the sick person well; the Lord will raise them up. If they have sinned, they will be forgiven. Therefore confess your sins to each other and pray for each other so that you may be healed. The prayer of a righteous person is powerful and effective."
>
> — JAMES 5:15-16 NIV

Lord, thank You for making us righteous through Your shed blood on the cross. Give us faith to pray and believe for healing.

Chapter 13

A Place of Peace

As the third day dawned after the attack on Landen, a nurse named Tammy entered our lives, introducing different protocols. I had grown accustomed to the sweet and tender nature of our nurse from the prior two days, so initially, it was challenging to accept this change.

I aimed to create a peaceful and comforting environment in Landen's hospital room. I applied lavender essential oils to his feet, filling our room with the soothing aroma. My mom brought a small lamp from home to cast a warm glow and replace the harsh overhead lights. I played instrumental worship music to fill the room with joy and bring life to the atmosphere. We also posted Bible verses and declarations of faith up on the walls.

Kari Hoffmann

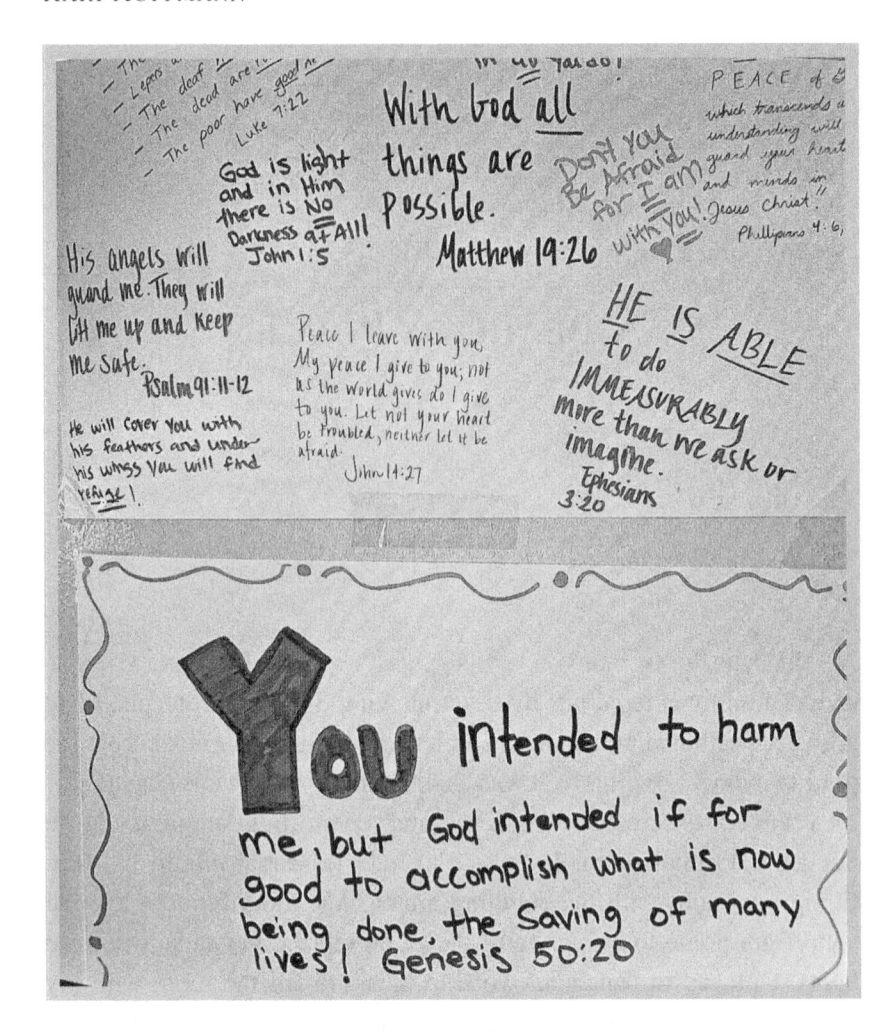

I wanted to create a healing space where only positive attitudes were allowed. I made it clear to visitors that crying, fear, and anger were not welcome in Landen's room. Anyone who needed to express those emotions was encouraged to do so in the hallway.

My instinct was to maintain a bustling and lively environment, as it provided me with a sense of reassurance. However, this clashed with Tammy's approach because she emphasized the importance of a quiet, structured atmosphere.

Tammy explained that while the previous days had been filled with hooting and hollering to keep Landen fighting, now was the time for a more tranquil setting. She emphasized allowing Landen to rest and deeply heal, urging me to be gentle while rubbing his feet or simply hold them instead.

Tammy implemented rules to limit the number of visitors in Landen's room to three. She stressed the need for whispering and quietness to create an environment of peace and tranquility. She even made a sign "Quiet Zone" and taped it to the door.

I struggled with this shift, which went against my instincts and what I believed was best for Landen. However, my perspective shifted as I began to engage with Tammy and witness the positive impact of the new approach. I started to appreciate Tammy for making the difficult decision to change our beliefs about Landen's care. I realized her decisions were rooted in a genuine desire for what was best for Landen's healing and recovery.

With this newfound understanding, my worries about Tammy's presence in the room turned into gratitude for her guidance. I recognized the courage it took for her to assertively communicate the necessary changes to me and my family. Our shared goal of providing the most optimal environment for Landen's healing united us in our efforts, fostering mutual respect and appreciation.

Surrounded by an incredible care team and finding peace in God, we were ready for the next big task: Landen's third MRI.

"Listen to advice and accept discipline, and at the end you will be counted among the wise."

— PROVERBS 19:20A NIV

"Prayer is bringing your worries to God. Faith is leaving them there."

— AUTHOR UNKNOWN

Lord, please help us to lay our burdens, cares, and worries at Your feet and leave them there. You can handle them so much better than we can.

Chapter 14

Anointing with Oil

The morning of Landen's third MRI dawned—five days after the attack—and something extraordinary unfolded. My childhood pastor, Mac, and his wife, Lynne, came to Landen's room to pray and anoint him with oil before his final MRI, which would give us a final confirmation of the extent of his brain injury. The previous scans had offered some level of insight, but the inflammation had made it exceedingly challenging for Dr. Halverson to provide a full prognosis.

Dave knew he still couldn't bear to see Landen in such a broken state, but he didn't want to miss this significant moment. He devised a plan involving Matt, one of Landen's nurses whom Dave often confided in about Landen's condition while he walked the hallways.

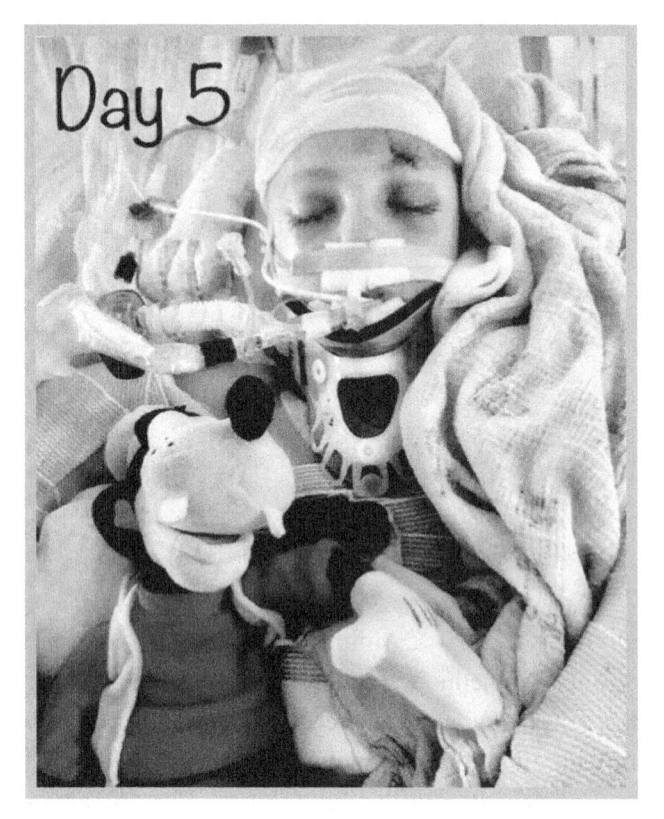

Landen lying in his hospital bed completely immobile, in a coma, with neck brace, casts, bandages, and tubes everywhere

Dave asked Matt to lead him past Landen's bed so Dave could keep his eyes closed. Matt guided Dave to a nearby couch, positioning him to face away from Landen. Dave could then join us during this critical moment but keep his eyes shut.

This marked the first time Dave entered Landen's room. His unwavering determination to be present with Mac and Lynne during this sacred time showcased his love and care for Landen and his devotion as a father.

When Mac and Lynne arrived, their presence brought me immense comfort. As they began to pray, their words echoed with power and conviction. They declared victory over the devil and proclaimed the healing power of Jesus.

"Lord, thank you for saving Landen's life! We believe this is the beginning of a supernatural miracle," Lynne began, her voice rising with conviction. "We claim complete victory for Landen in Jesus' name. The enemy will not prevail in this situation! Lord, thank You for restoring his body. May the doctors be guided by Your hand and let Your continued grace and healing power flow in this room."

Mac gently laid his hand upon Landen's chest and continued, "In the mighty name of Jesus, we come before You boldly, proclaiming Landen's body to be completely restored from the top of his head to the tips of his toes. We demand that the devil take his hands off this precious child. We command him to get behind us. Satan, you have no place here. We plead the blood of Jesus over Landen's body. We declare that no weapon formed against us shall prosper. We command the devil to flee from us in the mighty name of Jesus."

Their comforting, familiar voices washed over me, reminding me we were not alone in this battle. In a beautiful display of our shared faith, we gathered around the Lord's table, partaking in a sacred communion that symbolized our connection to God.

Pastor Mac, a true beacon of unwavering faith, gently anointed Landen's head with oil, creating a holy atmosphere that enveloped the room as he said, "Just as Your Word commands, I anoint Landen with oil in Your name, Lord. I declare that Landen is healed by the stripes of Jesus Christ, and I ask You, Lord, to heal him." It served as a potent reminder that God guided us toward healing and restoration despite the difficulties and uncertainties.

We continued in prayer for several minutes, our voices rising and falling in turn as we petitioned God to bring healing to Landen. After the final "Amen," Lynne gathered me close in a hug as Mac went to Dave.

Pulling Dave to his feet, Mac led him outside Landen's room for a private conversation while Lynne and I joined them in the hallway at a distance.

In the hallway, Mac looked at Dave and started redirecting his focus past what he saw to the Word of God.

"Dave, you are walking through a horrible, traumatic situation, but you cannot allow that to be your focus. If you do, you will give the enemy room for his purpose to prevail. He will make this situation feel so overwhelming that you lose sight of the promises of God. You cannot let that happen."

Mac paused to let his words sink in, then continued, "The questions will come. You'll wonder why this happened to Landen, but you don't have to let your mind stay there. Use your words to keep your mind in check. Speak the truth of God's Word over Landen's life. Landen will live and not die and proclaim the good works of the Lord. His life will become a testimony of the Lord's miraculous healing power, God's forgiveness, and His grace."

Dave looked at Mac, letting the words soak in. It was as though the words were a healing salve to the questions and frustrations that Dave had been fighting against.

"Stand strong and use your thoughts and words to embrace God's promises. See Landen running, jumping, leaping, dancing, and praising God. The power of God will keep this from becoming an obstacle, and you will have your miracle. You will always be able to look at Landen and know that God answers prayers."

When they returned, there was a noticeable shift in Dave's demeanor. He carried himself differently, his gaze filled with renewed hope and determination. I knew Mac's words had struck a chord within him, urging him to stop focusing on the tragedy and instead focus on Landen's miraculous recovery.

As we waited for them to come to take Landen for his MRI, Pastor Jason, senior pastor at our current church, also visited us, offering a powerful prayer that further encouraged our hearts.

Surrounded by the prayers and love of so many wonderful people, we bravely walked into the basement of the hospital, where they had moved Landen for the MRI. Anticipation and nervousness filled the air. Dave, Mac, and Lynne left, so my mom and my cousin Brian—who is an emergency room doctor—were by my side, offering unwavering support and invaluable expertise during this pivotal moment. The echoes of the MRI machine reverberated through the hospital, serving as a constant reminder of the gravity of the upcoming test.

Together, we huddled in that basement room, clutching onto faith and drawing strength from our incredible support system. We understood that this third MRI would be decisive, providing us with a definitive understanding of the extent of Landen's brain injury.

A storm raged outside that day, accompanied by thunderous roars and pouring rain. The power of prayer enveloped us as numerous individuals worldwide fervently petitioned God on Landen's behalf. Landen's preschool and Bible study groups held him in their collective thoughts and prayers, while Katie's church in Washington joined in praying for his complete restoration. The dedication from our church community was truly overwhelming. Hundreds of thousands on social media indicated that they were praying for Landen. Prayer chains were forged, uniting countless individuals in devoted intercession.

With closed eyes in that basement room, we could tangibly feel the energy of those prayers blanketing us, providing solace and strength. Side-by-side, we clung to the belief that complete healing was possible, envisioning an MRI that would conclusively reveal no evidence of a brain injury. The collective strength of our faith and the resounding power of love surrounded us, propelling us amidst the uncertainty, and anchoring our unshakable hope for Landen's future.

Finally, the moment we had been waiting for arrived. Dr. Halverson emerged from the MRI room, a smile lighting up his face. Instantly, I knew that this was good news.

"You guys, it looks good. From a brain standpoint, his injuries look like he fell off a bike." He presented a computer screen showcasing images of Landen's brain.

The pictures revealed small areas of injury towards the front and back. I learned brain tissue cannot heal or regenerate, but luckily, the parts of Landen's brain responsible for speech, walking, and personality showed no impairment.

Dr. Halverson continued, saying, "My hypothesis is that Landen's body acted as a protective cushion, like an airbag, taking the forceful impact of the landing and safeguarding his brain from severe damage. Landen may have even unintentionally collided with another surface on his descent, which unexpectedly served as a buffer, breaking his fall and preventing further harm to his brain."

But we would later learn, after reviewing footage of the incident, that Landen had hit the ground floor without hitting or landing on anything else first. It confirmed beyond any doubt that this sequence of events was a remarkable and unexplainable MIRACLE. Nothing had broken Landen's fall even the slightest little bit.

This is a current photo taken from the actual floor where Landen was thrown. The X superimposed over the photo shows the approximate location where he was thrown. He landed on the ground floor with nothing breaking his fall.

My son was thrown forward over the railing with some force. He then underwent a 39-foot freefall, landing directly on a concrete floor. We even checked with the mall to verify the height, and it is exactly 39 feet and 7 inches.

MIRACLE AT THE MALL

This is a current photo taken from the third floor railing with the camera angled downward toward the ground. It gives a sense of the height of the drop.

People can break their neck or their back falling from a 6-foot ladder. People can even die from falling as they walk or stand, especially if they hit their head.

The absence of anything at all that could have broken his fall reinforced that Landen had been miraculously protected from devastating brain and organ injuries. We were witnessing something truly extraordinary. This circumstance defied the boundaries of our human understanding, reminding us that there's something beyond the rational and logical.

God intervenes in our lives to show us that miracles exist and that they are beyond our comprehension. It's as if He wants to make completely clear that *only He* has the power to perform such remarkable acts.

If we define a miracle as something that defies all logical, rational, and natural explanation, then no one can convince me that God doesn't perform miracles. We have lived one.

Hearing Dr. Halverson's words, a surge of relief washed over me. An indescribable burden lifted from my shoulders. I recognized with certainty that when Landen woke up, he would still possess the same vibrant personality, speech, and mobility that made him who he was.

I immediately called Dave to share the incredible news. "Dave, he's going to be okay!" I cried with joy as he answered my call on the first ring. "Dr. Halverson said the brain injuries look like he fell off a bike! He'll be able to walk and talk and be himself again. We're getting our boy back!"

The release of relief overwhelmed him, and I immediately heard him break down in tears. "Kari, we're getting our boy back!" he said, joining me in joy. I heard him move through the house to where his parents were, and he said, "Brace yourselves. Landen is going to be okay! His MRI looked great!" I heard their cries of relief and joy, and my heart felt so light.

The weight of uncertainty lifted, and a sense of new beginnings flooded my being. A deep sigh of relief escaped my lips, and for the first time since the attack, I could breathe. The journey of healing—from broken bones to the pains of rehabilitation—suddenly felt bearable. Landen's brain was deemed intact and unharmed. The thought of getting my precious son back, seeing him emerge from this ordeal with his essence intact, filled me with immeasurable anticipation.

We embarked on our journey's next chapter with a newfound hope and optimism. As we awaited Landen's awakening, I held onto the profound knowledge that he would return to us unchanged in the ways that truly mattered. The long road to recovery lay ahead, but the world's weight lifted off of our shoulders, allowing us to step forward into this new beginning with determination and gratitude.

"Is anyone among you sick? Let them call the elders of the church to pray over them and anoint them with oil in the name of the Lord."

— JAMES 5:14 NIV

"Now then, stand still and see this great thing the LORD is about to do before your eyes!"

— 1 Samuel 12:16 NIV

Declare this with me: *I have a big God that can do big miracles!*

Chapter 15

Another Attack on Landen's Life

When Dave and I found out we were expecting twins, we lived in a cozy two-bedroom house. We were overjoyed to become parents and decided to prepare a nursery for our little ones. We excitedly wallpapered the room across the hall from ours and even built two cribs outside the nursery—only to realize they wouldn't fit through the door. We had quite the laugh as we had to disassemble and then rebuild them inside the nursery. Ah, the mistakes first-time parents make!

Everything seemed perfect for our babies' arrival until my cousin Courtney and her husband, Steve, mentioned that they were looking for a new house. During my baby shower, I had told everyone that our current house was sufficient, with the babies sharing a room. However, everyone knew we would need to move as the children grew or if we wanted to expand our family.

So Steve shared an intriguing idea with us—there was a short-sale house available across the street from the one they were interested in. Both houses conveniently had pools, which piqued our interest. We decided to check it out. It turned out that the occupants of the house needed to relocate quickly, and our current house was easily sellable. It seemed like the stars were aligning!

Without hesitation, we made an offer on the house, and it was accepted. These events felt like quite the whirlwind as we finalized everything and then swiftly moved in the day after I gave birth. Dave took charge, gathering our friends and family to help with the move while I was in the hospital for five days, recovering from the beautiful chaos of delivering twins and adjusting to life as a first-time mom.

It's amazing to think that we started our family and moved into a new house at the same time. But coming home to this wonderful new space was undeniably worth it. The twins never got to see the nursery we had lovingly prepared in our old house, but we replicated it exactly in our new home. Haden and Haley still shared a room, but as they grew, they'd have their own individual spaces. And, of course, we had an extra room ready and waiting for a third child whenever we decided we were ready for that next adventure.

Adjusting to life with twins was a whole new experience—we weren't the carefree individuals we used to be. It took a couple of years for us to feel like ourselves again as we navigated the sleepless nights and constant care required for our little ones. Despite feeling overwhelmed, we knew our family wasn't complete yet. In 2014, we welcomed Landen into our lives, and it felt like the missing piece had fallen into place.

When Landen turned two years old, Dave and I realized it had been a while since we had socialized with our friends. We decided it was time to plan a party and invited them over for a swim in our pool. We wanted to see how everyone had changed and grown, with their new little ones and babies in tow. During the party, I sat on the stairs with Landen and chatted with friends while the older kids played and dove for toys in the shallow end.

The party went on, and I saw a child at the bottom of the shallow end near the stairs. I initially thought it was Haden diving for toys, not realizing it was Landen. A dad noticed and quickly rescued him. Landen coughed and spat out water, but he was okay. We didn't know it at the time, but we should have taken him to the hospital due to the risk of something called "dry drowning."

Thankfully, Landen was okay, but I couldn't believe he had almost drowned right before my eyes. It was a wake-up call, and I immediately wanted everyone to leave.

Dave and I decided to avoid having pool parties with so many young kids present—the fear of drowning was too great for us. It forced us to realize that our lives had changed. We had three little ones to care for, and socializing with friends would have to wait. It took me a while to recover from the fact that Landen had come so close to losing his life that day. It shook me to the core, and I just wanted to keep my kids close to me, protecting them from any harm.

The following summer, Haden and Haley were in their last year of Pre-K and turning five years old. I invited Haden's best friend and his family over for a swim and some hotdogs on the grill. Dave was away on a work trip, but I assured him that it would be okay with just three additional guests. Reluctantly, he agreed, but I knew he wasn't entirely comfortable with me hosting people at the pool without him present. They arrived, and we had a great time swimming and playing. As we sat around to eat our hotdogs, the kids took off their wet puddle jumpers and sat in their towels, enjoying their meal.

Little did I know, Landen had quietly jumped into the deep end without my knowledge.

Suddenly, I felt a strange urge to turn my head toward the deep end; I believe it was an angel guiding me. There, I spotted Landen in the water without his floaties. In a split second, I realized what was happening, and without hesitation, I jumped into the pool, fully clothed, grabbing Landen just in time.

Dave just so happened to be pulling into the driveway at the exact moment, and he heard my terrified screams. Landen was coughing up a lot of water and crying terribly. It was much worse than the first time, and I knew I had to act swiftly. I placed him in the car, still soaked, and drove straight to the children's hospital to ensure he was alright. It was an out-of-body experience, and I couldn't help but think of how thankful I was to have him safe by my side.

After this second incident, I no longer wanted to swim—the fear of water with little ones became too much. I wanted to keep my kids protected in a bubble.

However, with a cabin by the lake and a house with a pool, swimming was a necessity in our family. Instead of succumbing to fear, I enrolled Landen in swimming lessons and made sure all three kids knew what to do if they fell into the pool or lake without a lifejacket. We practiced floating on their backs, yelling for help, and making their way to the edge.

Only when I was confident in their swimming abilities did I consider allowing others to join us for a swim. It required constant vigilance, counting heads, and being hyper-aware of everyone's whereabouts. Swimming wasn't as enjoyable for me anymore, but the kids loved it, so I knew we had to find a way to make it work.

I realize now that the devil had been relentlessly trying to harm Landen since before he was born, from uncertainties surrounding his early survival (viability via IVF), to the near-drownings, to the horrific attack at the mall. Satan knew the immense purpose God had for Landen's life. He understood that God would use Landen's story to open people's eyes and reveal His miracles, ultimately bringing thousands of unbelievers or struggling believers closer to Christ. The devil failed time and time again to take him out. God has the victory, and His divine plan will come to fruition.

All I can say now is, "But God..."

"I waited patiently for the LORD; he turned to me and heard my cry. He lifted me out of the slimy pit, out of the mud and mire; he set my feet on a rock and gave me a firm place to stand. He put a new song in my mouth, a hymn of praise to our God. Many will see and fear the LORD and put their trust in him."

— Psalm 40 1-3 NIV

"The LORD will keep you from all harm—he will watch over

your life; the LORD will watch over your coming and going both now and forevermore."

— Psalm 121:7-8 NIV

God, thank You for Your promise to watch over our lives and keep us from all harm. We give You praise for keeping Your promise in Landen's life. Let many see this and put their trust in You, Jesus.

Chapter 16

Resurrection Power

It was Easter Sunday, April 21st, nine days after the attack on Landen.

The last four days since Landen's MRI had been a blur of doctors, nurses, tests, facial surgeries, and fever. The medical professionals decided to keep him under sedation in the early days of his healing, but they were gradually lessening the dose as the days went by.

I listened to Pastor Mac's Easter sermon as I sat at the foot of Landen's hospital bed, gently holding his toes. It may seem an unconventional place, but it was my favorite spot. His life-support devices, like his breathing tube, brain drain, and IVs, prevented me from sitting by his head, so I nestled myself at the bottom of his bed, holding his precious feet close as I poured my heart into my journal.

> HAPPY EASTER-
> The King is ALIVE!
> Landen baby, the same King that raised Jesus from the dead is healing you right now! He loves each & everyone one of us so much. We are all His all we have to do is let him in ♥ Heaven will fight for you!

Pastor Mac's words echoed through the room, "Get in your prayer closet, send a spiritual arrow, and God will guide it into the enemy's camp to make him stop harassing you. Through Jesus' work on the cross, you are uncurseable and untouchable. Claim that in the name of Jesus!" I hummed in agreement, my head nodding with his words.

Suddenly, something truly extraordinary happened. Landen began to show signs of progress toward waking up. His beautiful eyes blinked briefly, and his tiny hands reached and grasped at the world around him.

"Landen, baby, can you hear me? Can you move your toes for Mommy?"

Indescribable joy filled my heart as his little toes began to move.

"That's so good, baby! I'm so proud of you!" I cried, tears filling my eyes.

In that profound moment, it felt as though he was right there with me—not in a coma completely disconnected from the world—but fully conscious and aware of my presence. Knowing Landen could hear me brought me so much comfort.

I called for the nurses to share in my joy and witness Landen's responses. There was a collective sense of hope and celebration—and the assurance that Landen's journey toward healing was going well.

Pastor Mac's sermon continued to play in the background as members of Landen's medical team entered the room to assess his condition. I believe Landen, even in his comatose state, responded to Pastor Mac's familiar voice, as well as the biblical truth Pastor Mac was speaking. Landen's response was a testament to his indomitable spirit and a source of immense pride and gratitude for me. I felt genuinely connected to him as if we were sharing that Easter Sunday, united in our unwavering faith.

As I sat in that hospital room, I thought about what I had imagined Easter Sunday would be like a few weeks earlier. I had already hidden all of the Easter basket items for the kids in my closet and bought Haley's Easter dress, but now I wouldn't be there to join in the festivities. It was up to my cousin Courtney to gather all the items and assemble the Easter baskets with candy and new spring toys. Dave stepped into the role of the Easter Bunny, something he didn't normally do, engaging in our regular yearly activities of leaving out carrots as a snack and creating Easter Bunny footprints around the house. Haley wore her Easter dress but adamantly refused to let anyone touch her hair, so it was left down and slightly messy.

Yet, even though the day wasn't like anyone planned, it still became a heartwarming memory for all of us.

A kind-hearted soul, a dear friend of Steve and Courtney's, orchestrated a truly magical day. He was a gifted chef and offered to cater a meal at Steve and Courtney's house for my family to be able to eat an Easter meal with them. Dave, the twins, and Courtney's family were blessed to be together without worrying about shopping for groceries or cooking. All of the dishes, even the desserts, was prepared with care, considering the dietary restrictions of our little ones. The thoughtfulness was nothing short of remarkable. I was comforted knowing they were all at home celebrating Easter together, enjoying the gift of life and good food.

As I sat by Landen's side in the hospital, I felt an overwhelming wave of peace wash over me. The realization that Easter would be enjoyed by my family at home brought immense comfort to my weary heart. Leaving Landen's side never crossed my mind.

I read *How to Catch the Easter Bunny* out loud to Landen. It's an Easter book that someone must have sent in one of the countless care packages we received from all over the world. This became another cherished moment as I shared this cute kid's story with my precious boy, even though he couldn't respond verbally.

As I sat that afternoon, I was overwhelmed with gratitude for the resurrection power of Jesus and the hope we find in celebrating Easter. I firmly believed the same King who conquered death was at work within us, even in those challenging moments. The Bible tells us that if we know the Lord Jesus, the same Spirit who raised Him from the dead lives in us. Not only that, but He gives life to our bodies! I held onto the conviction that Heaven was fighting for us, and all we needed to do was ask for and believe in God's power.

"He is not here, for *He has risen*."

— MATTHEW 28:6A AMP EMPHASIS ADDED

"And if the Spirit of him who raised Jesus from the dead is living in you, he who raised Christ from the dead will also give life to your mortal bodies because of his Spirit who lives in you."

— ROMANS 8:11 NIV

Hallelujah! He is risen. Death is defeated, and love has won! Lord, thank You for conquering death and the grave by the power of Your resurrection. We believe that you give life to our mortal bodies!

Chapter 17

Waiting

During the two weeks following the attack on Landen, there were moments of hope, followed by moments of disappointment. The doctors suggested removing the breathing tube, only to change their minds later. It became extremely frustrating to wait—especially when Landen seemed eager to wake up but was given more medicine to keep him asleep.

I couldn't bear to see him in this state; it felt like torture.

Even worse, the changing of doctors during their three-day shifts often led to different opinions and plans, adding to the uncertainty.

Not once, but twice, they shifted gears regarding removing the tube and letting him come out of his medically-induced coma. The second time they changed their minds about this, I couldn't hold back my emotions.

Breaking down in tears, I pleaded with the attending doctor, "Please, let Landen wake up! I can see in his eyes that he wants to wake up."

Fortunately, my cousin Brian, who is a trauma surgeon, was there to support me. Together, Brian and I convinced the doctor that it was finally time to remove the tube.

However, removing it was a multi-step process. First, the brain drain had to be taken out gradually, with the flow closing off little by little over several days. Finally, the tube was removed on April 25th, at 7:20 am, 13 days after the attack on Landen.

I woke up at 5:00 am to sit in Landen's bed at his feet and pray, anticipation and anxiety mingling in my heart. *Lord, steady the doctors' hands.*

Help the tube removal go smoothly.

Please bring Landen out of this sleep so I can talk to my sweet boy again.

I was thrilled at the thought of him being awake and sharing this momentous occasion with him. *When the tube comes out, I will be able to sit in his bed with him, by his face, and finally hold him! He can look at me, talk to me, and tell me how he's feeling,* I thought.

I wanted him back so badly, and it was hard to be patient, but I tried to sit silently with him in that quiet, peaceful morning while the sun came up.

The doctors arrived to remove the brain drain. I couldn't help but shed tears of both relief and hope. This marked the beginning of the waiting game for Landen to awaken fully. The doctors explained that once they turned off the medication, it was up to Landen to wake up—a process that could take a significant amount of time. No one knew for sure how long.

Thankfully, Landen quickly began to stir, opening his eyes and moving slowly as the medicine began to wear off. With Landen regaining consciousness, they could begin the process of removing his breathing tube.

I, along with my mom and dad, eagerly waited for the extubating process as the respiratory team closely monitored Landen's breathing through CPAP trials to determine when he could start taking breaths on his own. It was a painstakingly slow process, and I found it incredibly difficult to witness, and to stay patient.

As Landen slowly regained consciousness, the medical team asked, "Landen, do you want us to take your breathing tube out?"

My heart squeezed as he nodded his tiny head in agreement.

"You're right, baby! I think it's time to get that breathing tube out.

Mommy can't wait to talk to you!" I said, encouraging both him and the medical team to move forward.

However, the doctors wanted him to fight a little longer, just as a newborn baby is encouraged to take their first breath independently. The process continued for an hour despite Landen's readiness, though it could have taken much longer. The frustration of watching Landen struggle to communicate his willingness while the tube remained in place was overwhelming.

Finally, they pulled the tube out. I could see that Landen was in considerable pain, his dry throat making it difficult to swallow. He was groggy and could not speak. He was sweating, coughing, and wincing.

Yet, amidst it all, I could see a slight smile when I kissed him and told him, "Mommy is here." This was a sign that Landen was genuinely awake and with me.

After they removed the tube, I finally had the opportunity to sit with him at the top of his bed. It was a significant step forward. However, Landen was in a broken, weakened state and heavily medicated for the pain. Although I had him there with me, he wasn't himself. He tried to speak, but the words didn't come out clearly.

Landen's frustration was evident when I mentioned that he had casts on his legs. He yelled, "No!" angry that he couldn't move his limbs. I tried my best to make him more comfortable, but his anger weighed heavily on me.

It took Landen a while to get a word out. When he did, it was not normal speech. This worried me, and I couldn't understand why he struggled to talk. His first words were slow and laborious, saying, "Baaaaaath" and "iiiiiiiiiPad."

I knew what he was asking for. At home, our nightly routine included bathing, changing into pajamas, and spending time with his iPad. It deeply saddened me that I couldn't give him what he was trying to ask for. I explained why he couldn't have those things, emphasizing that he still had me, books, and other games to enjoy. But deep down, I wished I could fulfill his requests.

He was thirsty and craved ice chips, so I gave him small sips, taking it slow to ensure he could swallow well. The taste of the ice chips delighted him, and he eagerly asked for more. As much as I wanted to give him what he desired, the nurses instructed me to proceed cautiously. Landen needed to relearn how to swallow, and we had to take it easy with his healing because he still had severe damage to his face.

The doctors provided laxatives to help his body recover and get things moving. As a result, Landen had quite a few bowel movements back-to-back, and it was a challenging ordeal to clean up the mess. Rolling him over onto his side was incredibly painful for him, and then we had to change all the sheets underneath him before rolling him back —only to repeat the process a short time later.

Caring for him during this time seemed to me like a full-time job for the medical staff, and it wasn't easy for me either, but I understood that his body needed to clear out the medications and do its job. I embraced my role in supporting and encouraging Landen each time the nurses attended to the cleaning process.

I had let Dave know earlier that day that Landen was awake, and he was on his way to the hospital, ready to see him.

"Daddy knows you're awake and can't wait to see you. He'll be here after he drops Haden and Haley off at school," I assured Landen.

Although he didn't smile, he nodded, indicating that he wanted Dave to be there.

When Dave walked into the hospital room, seeing Landen for the first time since before the attack, I saw him break and come together again all at once. Although Dave's shoulders carried incredible weight, he smiled at Landen.

"Landen, I'm so proud of you. Daddy is so happy to see you," he said. Dave sat by his bed and talked to him, although I could tell he was afraid to touch Landen's small, fragile body, still bandaged and connected to wires.

It was a bittersweet day, filled with both joy and difficulty.

That night, I got to sleep in Landen's bed, right by his head, holding him tightly all night. I rested with joy and gratefulness, relieved to have my arms around my precious boy.

Good night, sweet Landen. You are safe, and I cherish having you awake. Sleep well, my sweet baby, I thought as I slipped into sleep.

"I wait for the Lord, my soul waits, and in his word I hope."

— Psalm 130:5 ESV

"But let patience have its perfect work, that you may be perfect and complete, lacking nothing."

— James 1:4 NKJV

Lord, thank You for the opportunities You give us to wait for You. Give us strength, patience, and faith while we wait. Help us to let patience complete its perfect work in us. Let us be comforted by the fact that You are eagerly waiting to give us what we're asking for, even though we need to go through Your healing process first.

Chapter 18

Controlling the Narrative

The next morning, I found myself awake before the sunrise, sitting in Landen's bed as he tried to catch a little more sleep after a rough first night out of sedation. As I lay there reflecting on God's goodness, Cheryl, our new day nurse, arrived.

"Hi, I'm Cheryl," she said as she entered the room with a big smile. "It's so nice to meet you. Landen is the talk of the hospital, so I'm glad I'm getting a chance to help him get better."

"It's nice to meet you, too," I responded as she started bustling around the room, checking Landen's chart and machines.

"I have a five-year-old son, too. I just can't imagine." Cheryl paused, her hand to her heart. "I was actually at the mall the day it happened, although I didn't see it. I'm glad to see Landen is beginning to heal."

I thanked her for her kind words. It touched my heart to see how much she genuinely cared for Landen.

As I sat there, I got a text message. For the first time, I learned the name of the man who threw Landen: Emmanuel.

Strangely enough, when we were asked to develop a code word for visitors to enter Landen's room the first week, I didn't feel particularly attached to any specific word. So, Katie, who was present when we were asked to choose a code word, suggested using "Emmanuel" because it means "God is with us." I didn't think much about it at the time, so I agreed. When I discovered that it was the same name as the man responsible for hurting Landen, tears began to stream down my face.

Cheryl noticed my distress and asked, "What's wrong?"

"I just found out the name of the man who did this to Landen: Emmanuel. We've been using that as our code word so our family and friends can get into the hospital to see us. I had no idea."

"Oh, my goodness. I would change that if I were you." Cheryl responded, shock on her face. "Is there another word you could use?"

One word immediately came to mind that I had been holding onto through Landen's healing journey: PERFECT. "Yes, I know the perfect one," I said, smiling.

I haven't really dwelled on this coincidence over the last few years, but I did always find it strange that the word chosen for visitors to see Landen was the name of the man who caused him harm. Later on, I reflected on this and realized that God was trying to convey a powerful message: Even through the terrible actions of this man named Emmanuel, God was with us.

In moments like this, it would be easy to let the enemy control the narrative. That's when we have to dig in, speak words of faith, and let God control the narrative by seeing things from His perspective, and believing His promises.

I was reminded of the countless miracles and signs from God that had manifested throughout this journey, from the nurses who rushed to his aid immediately after he landed to the minimal brain damage that would leave his personality and mobility intact. God's presence is everywhere if we take the time to notice and appreciate it.

After Cheryl left that morning, I took out my journal, feeling incredibly loved by my Heavenly Father. Sitting there in the dark morning with the beautiful sunrise outside the window, I wrote about how the man who harmed Landen must have experienced something truly terrible in his life to want to hurt such a sweet little boy.

I didn't feel any hate toward him because Jesus shielded me from those emotions and surrounded me with His overwhelming love, leaving no room for anything else.

I recognized that this is how humans giving in to temptation and sinfulness operate—repaying evil with hatred—but I was firmly rooted in my faith. I know God does not promote hate. As stated in John 13:34 (NIV), "Love one another. As I have loved you, so you must love one another."

I was not in a position to hate or to personally pass final judgment on anyone. The action was wrong and evil—we can all certainly make that judgment. But I cannot judge the person. I knew God would have the final say and deliver a just punishment for the evil that was committed. I refused to let negative emotions poison my mind because indulging in them would only harm Landen and myself.

The enemy seeks to steal, kill, and destroy, but I wouldn't let him win in any aspect of my mind. James 4:7 tells us that Satan must flee when we submit ourselves to God and resist the devil. I refused to entertain even a fleeting thought of temptation from Satan. He wanted to tempt my mind, making me feel sorry for myself and Landen. He wanted me to hate the man responsible for Landen's pain, but I rejected that temptation. I chose life, love, healing, and faith.

I believed that to stay in faith, I also had to stay in obedience to God and His Word—not giving the enemy even a microscopic amount of ammunition to attack us with.

Landen began to stir as daylight broke through the windows.

Leaning in close, I said, "Good morning, baby. Would you like a popsicle or something to drink?"

The speech team assisting Landen with regaining his ability to talk and eat had mentioned that he could try having a popsicle today.

Landen nodded yes, so I requested they bring him one.

They arrived with a large rainbow popsicle, and Landen was overjoyed to have this treat. They taught him how to take minor licks and gentle sucks to enjoy it. He couldn't bite for another 6-8 weeks due to his broken jaw. Landen adored the popsicle, managing to finish the entire thing. It brought me such joy to see him enjoying the popsicle when I knew he was suffering so much pain.

He also got a chance to try applesauce and eagerly asked for more. This made me believe we could remove the feeding tube from his nose if he continued eating independently. Witnessing his happiness brought me great joy.

The occupational therapy team checked to see if he was ready to play. However, he was still experiencing chills and fever. Another issue is that he was frequently falling asleep for short periods throughout the day.

Finally, we managed to get some sleep that night. The doctors discontinued the nighttime feedings, allowing us to rest. With no more force-feeding and the ability to drink and consume soft foods, we were beginning to feel a sense of normalcy. We were on the right path.

Dr. Halverson stopped in to tell me that kids with concussions sleep a lot and have headaches. He explained that these symptoms can go on for months.

I immediately said, "We've got this, and I do not believe it will take that long."

I knew Jesus was holding Landen in His hand.

I told Landen, "We can do this. I love you so much, baby."

"I create the fruit of the lips: Peace, peace to him who is far off and to him who is near," Says the LORD, "And I will heal him."

— Isaiah 57:19 NKJV

"As for me, this is my covenant with them," says the Lord. "My Spirit, who is on you, will not depart from you, and my words that I have put in your mouth will always be on your lips, on the lips of your children and on the lips of their descendants—from this time on and forever," says the Lord.

— Isaiah 59:21 NIV

Thank You, Lord, for the opportunity to partner with You by staying in faith and declaring Your promises!

CHAPTER 19

NOT TODAY, SATAN!

IN THE INITIAL HOURS AND DAYS AFTER LANDEN WAS BORN, I HAD A sense of something being off. Despite being overwhelmed with exhaustion, I cherished the moments of holding him in my arms and nursing him every few hours while my parents or Dave managed the spirited two-and-a-half-year-old twins. I was recovering from a second C-section, which was a tough and prolonged process.

It was during this time that I was diagnosed with celiac disease, which is an autoimmune disease that affects the small intestine. When a person with celiac disease eats gluten, the immune system responds by attacking the villi, which are small, fingerlike projections that line the small intestine. Villi are crucial for helping your body absorb nutrients, so when they become damaged, your body will have trouble properly absorbing nutrients.

I was advised to have Haley and Haden tested as well since the condition can be hereditary, and I likely had it during my pregnancy with them. To my surprise, Haden tested positive.

After conducting biopsies to confirm the blood test results, we knew for certain that Haden and I had celiac disease, while Haley was diagnosed with a gluten allergy.

It felt like my family was under attack. I was nervous about how this would affect us for the rest of our lives. I needed to figure out a whole new way of life. I hadn't even heard of celiac disease, and now Haden and I both had it. After crying and processing many emotions, I knew I needed to get a handle on the situation and come up with a plan of action, educating myself and learning to manage our new lifestyle.

My mom and sister stepped in and helped me clean everything out of my kitchen that may have gluten on it, like my toaster oven, cutting boards, and pans. We also cleaned out my fridge and cupboards of all things gluten and went shopping for all new foods we could eat safely. My mother-in-law, Sharon, bought me my first easy-cooking gluten-free cookbook, and I got serious about our health.

I learned to cook in a whole new way, and I also hired a gluten-free nutritionist to help guide me on our new way of life.

"No, not today, Satan!" is what I stood on during that life-altering time. I had read that the word *devil* means 'deceiver.' I bought a sign that said, "No, not today, Devil!" and put it on my desk next to my bed. I was not going to let him deceive us. This was a battle against evil, so I meditated on Ephesians 6:11 (NIV): "Put on the full armor of God, so that you can take your stand against the devil's schemes."

I needed to take my family back and come out stronger on the other side, so that's what I did. I didn't let Satan take us down the path of worry and uncertainty. I planted my feet firmly on the ground and asked God to help me make a way when I saw no way.

I occasionally found myself thinking about how Haden will have to manage celiac disease throughout his life, particularly during his college years when others might order pizza or get fast food that he can't have. These thoughts made me anxious, as I wondered how he would cope. However, I quickly captured those fears and cast them away, refusing to let them take hold.

In general, I strive to cast my worries onto the Lord and resist the urge to pick them back up. Some days, this is easier than others; it's a continual battle that must be fought. I think that these kinds of battles throughout my life prepared me for the war I would have to fight for Landen.

"Cast all your anxiety on him because he cares for you."

— 1 Peter 5:7 NIV

"The weapons we fight with are not the weapons of the world. On the contrary, they have divine power to demolish strongholds. We demolish arguments and every pretension that sets itself up against the knowledge of God, and we take captive every thought to make it obedient to Christ."

— 2 Corinthians 10:4-5 NIV

Lord, please help us to fight our battles the way You intend, through prayer, faith, spiritual gifts, and the declaration of Your promises over our lives.

Chapter 20

Surprising the Doctors

I was more determined than ever to bring a smile to Landen's face. But no matter what I did, no matter how many funny faces I made or silly jokes I told, he remained stubbornly unmoved. The doctors suggested using a thumbs-up to signify agreement since Landen's speech abilities were challenged. He quickly embraced this method of communication, using it to interact and convey his thoughts without speaking a word.

I realized Landen needed some rest, as he had been working tirelessly to recover. We decided to give him a break from our constant efforts to engage him. Although he wouldn't communicate verbally, Landen found comfort and support in the presence of our visitors, such as his grandparents.

Landen's appetite diminished as the days passed, leaving me questioning why he was losing interest in food. It wasn't until they removed the feeding tube that we discovered the impact of the sedation medication. Landen had been acting unlike himself, and I couldn't help but feel frustrated at his lethargic disposition. I kept asking why he was like this, but no one could say for sure.

Landen was eventually transferred to a different hospital section on the same floor, no longer under constant nursing care. This was a sign of progress, and it gave me hope that we would soon be able to leave the hospital altogether. Representatives from Gillette, a rehabilitation hospital facility, met with me to discuss transitioning there, which was a hopeful and exciting prospect for the future.

Meanwhile, letters poured in from various places all over the world. I had no energy to read them, but other family members informed me. These messages of love and support provided much-needed comfort, reminding us that we were not alone in this journey. A friend from church sent me a song called "Raise a Hallelujah," which became my anthem as I faced each new day while holding Landen close.

My family also told me an incredible display of support unfolded at the mall in the very spot he had landed. People from all walks of life came forward, offering their love. Stuffed animals, toys, cards, flowers, and sweet treats multiplied, forming a sea of well-wishes. Someone volunteered to collect the stuffed animals at the end of each day to donate them to local charities and schools, but more would keep coming. It was a testament to the power of compassion.

Outpouring of support at the mall

Amidst the emotional rollercoaster, significant milestones were occurring. Another MRI confirmed that Landen's brain was healing well after the drain removal. He also underwent surgery to reset the broken bones in his arm.

Landen's first arm procedure involved setting the bones in place using complex casts that were very uncomfortable and large.

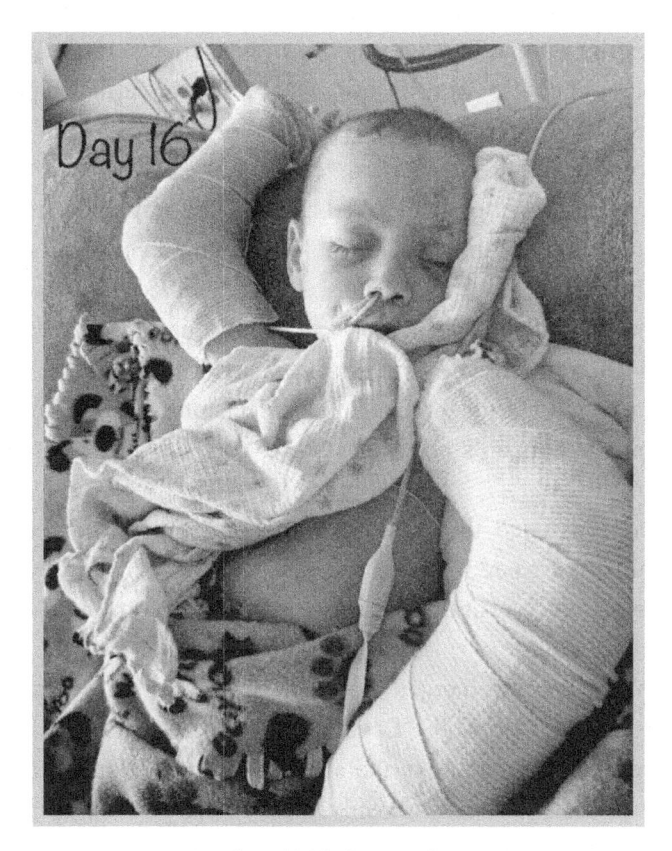

Landen with his first set of casts

While these didn't bother him during his coma, he needed more comfortable casts now that he was awake. The orthopedic surgeon, Dr. Engels, intended to remove the large casts and assess the healing of his shattered elbows. The bones in his elbows were held together by screws, and Dr. Engels was checking if Landen had healed enough to remove those screws before fitting him with smaller, more comfortable casts.

Dr. Engels was a Christian and made sure we knew about his faith. In the pre-op room, he sat down with me, my mom, and my dad, sharing a story about his recent vacation in California. While at the beach, he mentioned he was from Minnesota, and people asked if he had heard about the boy thrown from the balcony at the mall. He confirmed that he had and explained that Landen was one of his patients. He began to tear up, expressing how this miracle story had profoundly affected people all over the world. He went on, saying, "I feel so honored to know you and have the opportunity to care for Landen."

Before the surgery my dad asked him, "Can I pray for you?"

Dr. Engels said, "Absolutely, yes. I'd love to pray with all of you."

The three of us bowed our heads, and my dad led the prayer. "God, thank You for saving Landen. I ask that Your presence be in the operating room with Dr. Engels. Let Landen's bones be perfectly restored, provide clarity for Dr. Engels' decisions. Show him the best ways to repair Landen's body, and place Your hand of blessing upon his work."

As we concluded the prayer, Dr. Engels smiled and thanked us before going to prepare for the surgery.

We settled in to wait out the surgery in peace, comforted by God's hand on the situation.

When Dr. Engels emerged from the surgery room, he had a huge smile on his face. He said, "Landen is healing remarkably well. Not only were we able to remove the screws, but he no longer needs any type of arm casts! Instead, we only provided removable wrist braces, which he'll have to wear for the next six weeks. God is good!"

We praised God for another miracle—a comforting sign from Him, reassuring us that He held us in the palm of His hand.

Landen's healing arms gave me renewed hope, believing we would soon be discharged from the hospital. Though we knew Landen's leg still required several weeks to heal fully, I held onto the belief that our time in the hospital was coming to an end.

Courtney and Lindsay brought celebratory pizza to share in Landen's room while he slept soundly. We whispered about the healing miracle we had witnessed and the imminent homecoming we anticipated.

However, I struggled to eat full meals, knowing Landen couldn't enjoy food.

It was the same for Dave.

After he fed the twins and settled them down for the night, he would light a candle for Landen and go over Landen's daily progress with Steve or Brian.

We were adjusting to this new normal together, and we hoped brighter days were ahead.

> "Great is the Lord and most worthy of praise; his greatness no one can fathom. One generation commends your works to another; they tell of your mighty acts. They speak of the glorious splendor of your majesty—and I will meditate on your wonderful works. They tell of the power of your awesome works—and I will proclaim your great deeds. They celebrate your abundant goodness and joyfully sing of your righteousness."
>
> — PSALM 145:3-7 NIV

> "Every good gift, every perfect gift, comes from above. These gifts come down from the Father, the creator of the heavenly lights, in whose character there is no change at all."
>
> — JAMES 1:17 CEB

Thank You, Lord, for the opportunity to share what You have done!

Chapter 21

Worldwide Prayer, Love, & Support

God brought so much good out of this situation.

One of the most moving aspects of this whole ordeal was the overwhelming amount of prayer, love, and support shown to us by our fellow man.

We had such an outpouring of support in the form of letters, cards, gifts, and care packages that it became overwhelming for the hospital. Some friends of ours set up a PO box to try to help manage the massive influx of support and care.

We received letters and cards from all over the US and the world—even from places like Singapore and Africa. Many of them were sent by school groups, with each student in the class sending a letter in a packet, resulting in three to five thousand letters total. Courtney, Lindsay, Brian, and some other family members were responsible for sorting through and screening the letters.

While going through the letters, Brian came across one from the father of Jessica. Jessica was one of the nurses from the mall who helped with CPR immediately after Landen hit the ground. Recognizing the letter's significance, Brian set it aside.

Courtney brought the letter to the hospital and handed it to me, saying, "This is from Jessica's dad. She was one of the nurses who came to help Landen right after he hit the ground. It might be worth reading since you want to know who saved Landen's life."

I placed the letter in my Bible, not ready to read it. I didn't feel I had the energy to reach out and express my gratitude yet.

About a month went by and things progressed smoothly, so I removed the letter from my Bible and read it:

Dear Family of Landen,

I am very close to this situation because my daughter Jessica and her friend were the two nurses that got to your son at the mall and were doing CPR compressions and breaths on your son. They were walking at the mall and heard your screams for help. They went down the escalator from the second floor after seeing your son at the kiosk on first floor and began the CPR procedure, within about 1 minute, with their instinct and precision that I believe Yahuwah God gave them as you called out for prayer to all that were around. Jessica recalled you scream out to the devil that he was not going to take this one. As Jessica told me the story less than 2 hours later, I totally felt the Holy Spirit's anointing on this whole situation. I was shaken to my core by the power of the Holy Spirit. I went online and already saw the news reports going out worldwide. I made comments on many of the news reports asking for even more prayer for your son and you. I saw one report in England in a very short time. I totally know without question that Yahuwah God responded to these prayers that came out of you and expanded to so many.

My daughter Jessica was the one that gave you hugs and support while you watched these talented people work on your son after another took over for the chest compressions. She was trying to calm you so they could hear your son's responses to the treatment. Her friend continued to breathe into your son. I personally believe that these anointed nurses were instrumental in your son's recovery, and they were there as a direct result of your prayers and cries for help. Yahuwah God and His Spirit was all over this situation. I still feel it today, 10 days later.

Ironically both the nurses, Jessica and her friend, work at Children's hospital where your son is being treated. Jessica works in the Neonatal ICU and I forgot where her friend works. Maybe you have met them as they have been quietly asking about your son's status. I don't know about the privacy issues related to this, but when you are free to talk more about this, I welcome you to contact us.

Jessica lives in Bloomington. I work in my business in Burnsville. I can give you her number and she can get you her friend's number. I am sure they would like to meet you and Landen.

I continue to monitor this as a dad, and I know my God Yahuwah has your son in His hands and is going to use this situation for your faith to be expanded. I pray for your continued support. I see that the Go fund me page is doing very well.

I so honor you and your faith in the one true God and our Creator. Your powerful cry for prayers and help, I still feel as I write this letter.

It would make a powerful movie that would prove the power of Yahuwah in our lives. I was just thinking of the producers of the movie Unplanned may be interested in it. I am sorry if this is too forward. But I know it is what we need in this world.

The letter was incredibly moving. In that moment, I felt ready to learn about their experiences and meet the nurses. I wanted to hug them, listen to their stories, and thank them.

Since I knew they worked on another floor at the same hospital, I asked our social worker to arrange a meeting. I felt guilty for making them wait to see us, but I knew the immense emotions it would bring up, and I needed to be prepared. I was under the impression we might be leaving soon, so it felt like the right time. I asked the nurses to come to Landen's room that evening. They had expressed their desire to meet me, and I wanted to talk to them before we left.

But that day, Landen was having difficulty breathing, and they discovered fluid in his right lung. Dr. Wahoff planned to put a drain in to remove the fluid and have it tested. It was not supposed to be a big deal. The tube was to be removed after a few days, once we confirmed what kind of fluid it was. I did not like this, but the doctors reassured me it was just a hiccup. We would remove the drain in a few days and move to Gillette as planned.

However, after the hectic day and setback to our plans, I canceled the meeting with the nurses and asked for it to be rescheduled for another time.

The drain became a constant problem as it would often kink and not drain properly. Additionally, the dressing would frequently come off, as it was only held on by tape. Landen hated when they had to pull off the tape, but moving and reattaching the dressing was necessary. When Dave visited the hospital, he would cover his arms with tape and have Landen rip it off. He was demonstrating to Landen that he would go through the pain with him—they would go through it together—which provided some comfort to Landen. The drain also looked painful, as it was a large tube poking into his side, with the puncture wound visible on his skin.

The tube extended down the side of his bed into a box that measured the fluid. The fluid was yellow, and the drain sounded loud, like a water fountain. I couldn't believe something like this could be attached to him, especially for a few days.

Fortunately, our prayer warriors were praying over every single issue that arose. There was a Facebook prayer group called "Prayers for Landen" that had thousands of people join so they could stay updated and pray for Landen each day. There were in-person Bible studies and small groups regularly praying over Landen, and there were many email and text chains, GroupMe groups, etc.

Katie had one email and text chain with prayers and prayer requests going on regularly throughout this entire ordeal. Katie, along with the other ladies in the prayer chain, spoke faith, hope, and trust. They declared God's promises, reminding everyone of who God is, rather than focusing on the problems. Here is just one of the many prayer emails Katie sent out:

Good Morning,

Landen's chest tube put out a ton of fluid yesterday 240. Please pray that it is from all the fluids given at time of surgery and it will start to slow down. The doctors told Kari this morning that the fluid could have moved over to the other side of his chest. If that is the case, they might have to put another chest tube in that side as well. His mama is very upset about this. Please pray that Landen recovers from this painful surgery, all this chest tube output stops, and that all his cavities stay open. We still need to pray to the God of Miracles to rescue and save little Landen, and to comfort and strengthen his mom!

We are praying Psalm 130 today! "Out of the depths I cry to You, O Lord... let your ears be attentive to my pleas for mercy!"

Almighty God,

We praise You because You are mighty to save! We boldly come into Your throne room of grace and beg for mercy for Landen with this fluid. We all stand with our eyes fixed on You, Our Great God and Landen's Great Physician! We continue to place all of our hope and trust in You alone to rescue, save and help him. Most Merciful Father, Help him recover from this painful surgery, stop the fluid output with Your Mighty Hand and outstretched arm of steadfast love and plentiful redemption. We wait on You more than watchmen wait for the morning because we are all mothers and fathers too who want to see this precious child weaned from these machines and tubes in Your perfect timing and Your perfect way! We know these machines and tubes have been Your grace and mercy in sustaining his life! We thank You for all You have done for him through the power of The Holy Spirit working in and through our prayers and through so many people! We are persuaded that You are able to keep Landen and Kari safe in Your everlasting arms where there is love, redemption, hope and perfect peace! Continue to rescue and save Landen to the praise of Your glory for it is in the strong name of Jesus we ask boldly for all You have promised in Your precious Living Word! Thank You for the cross where Jesus made a way for us to come to You, O God, Father, Son and Holy Spirit... work together as You always do in this amazing rescue mission! The way You save all of us O God, is miraculous and amazing! You still are a Miracle working God! We love Kari and Landen! We know that no one loves them more than You do O God! Your ways are higher than our ways! We trust You! We love You! We place all of our hope in You! In the Strong Saving name of Jesus we pray for there is no other name given among men whereby we must be saved! Amen.

"I will give thanks to You, Lord, with all my heart; I will tell of all Your wonderful deeds." Psalm 9:1

Thank You God for all You have done!

Katie

The nurses expressed concerns about me being in his bed, worrying that I might accidentally kink the line or tug on it and cause him harm. However, leaving his bed was not an option. Landen wanted me there, and I wanted to be there, too. I sat on the opposite side of the drain, and when we slept, I made sure to be very still so that I could stay by his side. It was challenging, but we managed to make it work. Nonetheless, I couldn't wait for those three days to be over so that we could remove that awful thing from his body.

MIRACLE AT THE MALL

The following day, I told Landen I would give him 15 kisses if he would smile, and he did. He smiled so big! I showered him with kisses —what an excellent way to start the morning!

The sedation medicine had completely worn off, so I was happy to see Landen coming back to himself. Our plan for the day was to have him sit in the recliner for a little while and have Dave push him around in a wheelchair. This would be the first time Landen had gotten out of bed since the attack.

We patiently waited for Dave, and when he got there, we went for a walk and played "I Spy" in the hallway. Landen loved it, and we were all so happy to play games out and about. When we returned to the room, a package had just arrived from Maryland with a game called *Headbands*.

Landen was still in the wheelchair in our room when I put a card on his head with a picture of a cat. He was supposed to guess what it said, so I told him, "It says meow."

Landen's face lit up, and he said, "Caaa uh."

It was his first word in so long, and I was incredibly proud and happy. I jumped up, clapped, and cheered for him, unable to believe what had happened. I captured this moment on video and watched it repeatedly, then sent it to all my family members, who tearfully responded with much joy.

For the rest of the day, Landen continued to sit up, play with Play-Doh and toys, and enjoy being happy. He also said some words, although it was challenging to get him to talk. I would prompt him with questions. I made Play-Doh figures of everyone in our family except Dave, and then I asked Landen who was missing.

He excitedly exclaimed, "Daddy!"

Enjoying these simple moments of play and joy with Landen, I thought back on the day before the attack, when Haley, Haden, and Landen were home due to school being canceled because of a snowstorm. They wrecked the kitchen by creating "potions" using apple juice and other ingredients in small cups, resulting in a huge mess. When Dave discovered it, he was not pleased. He asked, "Who did this?"

Haley and Landen quickly ran to the next room, giggling and hiding under a table. Dave, following them, questioned, "Do you think this is funny?"

In a soft voice, Landen replied, "Yes, we think it's funny and tastes good."

I found it amusing and cleaned up the mess so Dave could continue working.

I wished we could return to those messy moments, and I longed for Landen to be able to make potions at home again. But for now, I could appreciate the light moments of fun and play we were able to have in the hospital.

So many of the care packages contained toys, games, and stuffed animals for Landen. One of them was full of Curious George stuff, including a plush of George himself, which Landen had fun with. Even though George is perhaps the most famous monkey in the world, Landen was calling him a puppy. He really likes puppies, so I thought George had simply become a puppy in his imagination.

Haden with Landen and his favorite stuffed animals

However, we would find out it was a little more complicated than that. The hospital sent a speech therapist to help Landen with his memory and words. Landen was always out of breath when he talked. His words would be jumbled together. He had to slowly think about what he wanted to say, then carefully form the words.

The speech therapist said that he would need to re-learn things he used to know, like what animals were. I had no idea he would have to start all over learning stuff like this. It scared me. What else did I not know? I had to function one day at a time. That was the only way to keep my peace.

Thankfully, the overwhelming amount of love, prayer, and support provided a strong feeling of reassurance. Knowing that people all over the world were praying for Landen was a massive help and comfort. And of course, God chooses to work through the prayers of believers. Seeing all the prayer support flowing in from everywhere gave me confidence that God was working mightily on Landen's behalf. Without all of those prayers, who knows where we would be today?

There were so many wonderful notes and cards that meant so much. One particular example was a drawing someone sent that said, "Landen's Angel" and had a hand drawn picture of an angel holding Landen. I have kept the picture to this day and it has meant so much to me. To the person who sent me the angel picture: thank you so much for taking the time to do that. It is very special to me.

KARI HOFFMANN

And thank you to everyone else who prayed, sent letters, formed prayer chains, sent gifts, and all the many other ways you supported us. I am forever grateful for every person who took the time to stop and pray for Landen, and to support us in various ways.

At this point in the journey, we were expecting the good news any day that we could leave the hospital to begin working for the next phase of Landen's recovery. Unfortunately, we did not realize at that time that more surprises lay ahead.

> "Indeed, we felt we had received the sentence of death. But this happened that we might not rely on ourselves but on God, who raises the dead. He has delivered us from such a deadly peril, and he will deliver us again. On him we have set our hope that he will continue to deliver us, as you help us by your prayers. Then many will give thanks on our behalf for the gracious favor granted us in answer to the prayers of many."
>
> — 2 CORINTHIANS 1:9-11 NIV

Thank You, Lord, for the believers around the world who rise up and pray when someone else is in crisis. Thank You for hearing and answering!

Chapter 22

When Hope Wears a Jersey

The days in the hospital all seemed to blend together—long, exhausting days filled with the sounds of beeping machines, nurses quietly coming and going, and me sitting by Landen's side, praying for answers. But in the middle of all that fear and confusion, we had moments that reminded us we weren't alone.

As the packages poured in from all over the world, every single one of them brightened our day. The excitement in those moments were like medicine—not the kind that dripped from IV poles or measured in syringes, but the kind that fills the heart with joy. My family would pick them up from the mailbox, open them, and bring the ones they thought Landen would enjoy most to the hospital. It was like Christmas morning, but instead of toys under a tree, we received gifts filled with hope from people we'd never even met.

Some of the most exciting packages came from Minnesota's professional sports teams. I'll never forget the day we opened a box from the Minnesota Vikings. Inside was a signed jersey from Adam Thielen—one of Landen's favorite players because he was from our very own city of Woodbury—and an official Vikings helmet covered with autographs from the whole team. It felt surreal, like a little piece of encouragement sent straight to us when we needed it most.

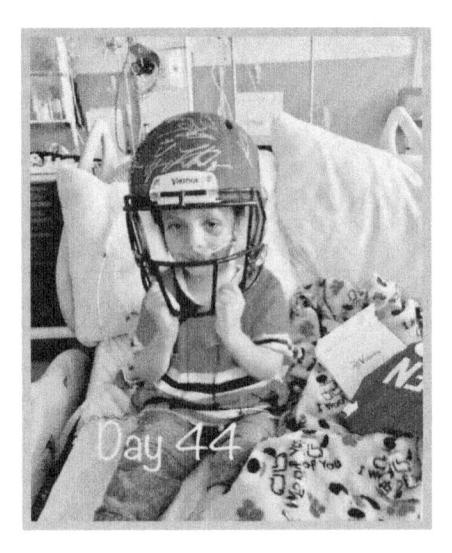

Landen posing with his official Minnesota Vikings autographed helmet

Another time, we received a basketball signed by the entire Minnesota Timberwolves NBA team. I could hardly believe how many names covered it. Even the Green Bay Packers—the Vikings' biggest rival—sent a signed football. It was incredible to see how sports could bring people together, no matter what team they cheered for.

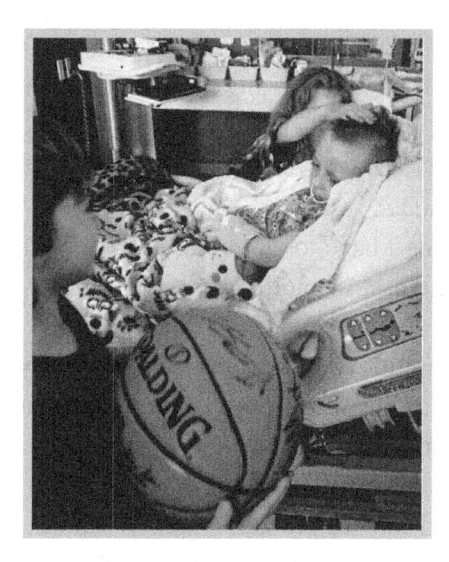

Haden holds the Minnesota Timberwolves autographed basketball beside Landen's bed. Haley is on the other side giving her brother some affection.

But our passion for other sports pales in comparison to our family's love for hockey, and hockey is by far Landen's favorite sport. He is crazy about the NHL team Minnesota Wild! So when we found out that Zach Parise—a star player for the Minnesota Wild—was at the hospital visiting kids, we couldn't believe it. Hospital staff told us that he wanted to come to our room and meet Landen personally.

Normally, I would've said yes without hesitation. I knew Haden, Landen's older brother, would've been thrilled too. But that day was different. Landen had just gone through a really tough procedure. He was in so much pain, and he was on so many medications that he could barely stay awake. We hadn't slept in days. I felt overwhelmed, exhausted, and honestly, like I had nothing left to give—not even for someone as special as Zach Parise.

So I told them, "Maybe." I needed to see how the day went. Could I get Haden out of school to be here? Would Landen be awake enough to enjoy the visit? Would I have the energy to hold it all together?

For hours, I went back and forth. But then I thought about how special this could be—a moment that Landen could look back on, even in the middle of all the pain. A memory of someone who took the time to show up when things were really hard. A picture of hope during one of our darkest days.

So finally, we said yes. Yes, we'd be honored to have Zach Parise visit us. Even though we were tired and broken, we realized that sometimes, you don't have to wait until everything is perfect to let joy in. Sometimes, the best memories are made right in the middle of the mess.

We are so thankful we pushed through and said yes to Zach Parise coming to visit Landen in the hospital. It turned out to be one of the most memorable and meaningful days of our journey.

Haden came straight from school, hockey stick in hand, along with some cards he had for Zach to autograph. When Zach arrived with his wife, Alisha, they were both incredibly kind—some of the sweetest people I've ever met. They walked in with a bit of hesitation, almost taken aback by the situation, but they quickly opened up and shared that they also had twins who were the same age as Landen. That connection immediately made the room feel warmer, more personal.

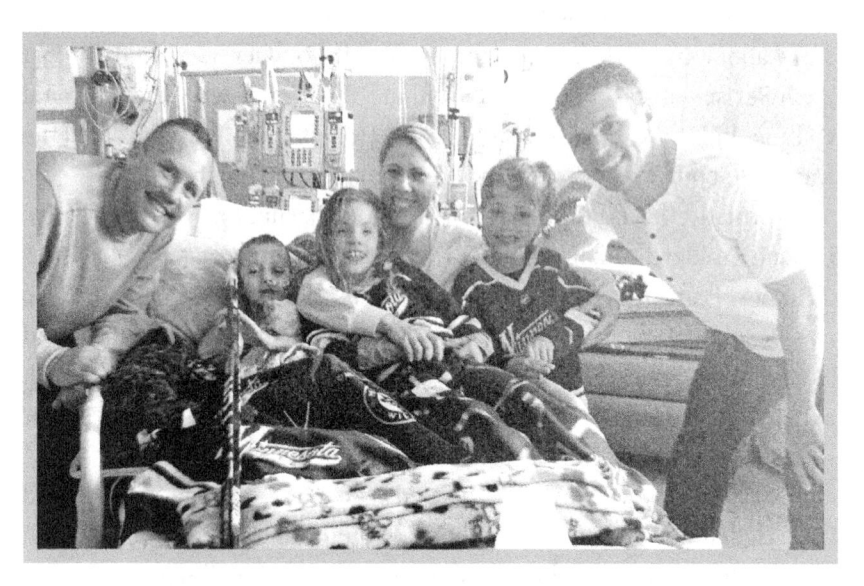

Zach Parise poses beside Landen's bed for a picture with our family

Their twins had even made cards for Landen. The cards were covered in stickers their twins stuck all over them, which made Landen smile. They handed the cards to Landen with so much love and compassion in their eyes.

It was clear that they weren't just there to make an appearance—they truly cared. Zach brought Landen one of his sticks that he actually used in a game. He also brought a jersey that Landen still proudly displays in his room. They posed for as many pictures as we wanted, signing everything Haden had brought with such patience and kindness. The visit was short and sweet, but it left an everlasting imprint on our hearts.

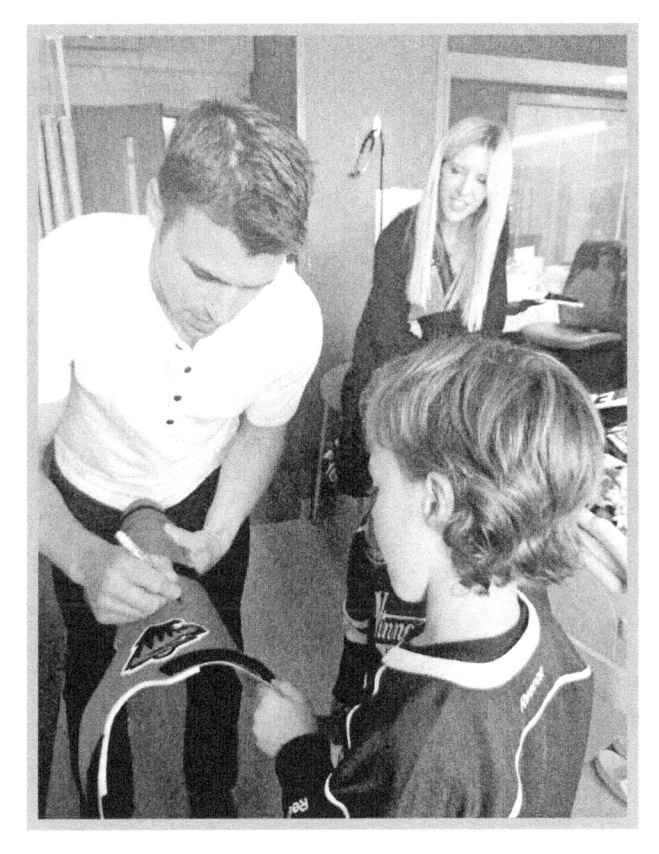

Zach and his wife, Alisha, during their visit to Landen. Zach is signing an autograph for Haden.

The autographed stick and jersey aren't just special because Zach is a great hockey player—they're treasures because of the heart behind them. They are reminders of the kindness, empathy, and genuine support Zach and Alisha showed us during one of the hardest times in our lives.

And it would turn out that this would not be the last time we would see Zach and Alisha!

"As a face is reflected in water, so the heart reflects the real person."

— Proverbs 27:19 NLT

"Love each other with genuine affection, and take delight in honoring each other."

— Romans 12:10 NLT

Lord, thank You for acts of kindness that lift us up when we need it most. Thank You for making us in Your image and putting kindness into our hearts so that we can show Your love to others.

Chapter 23

Jesus Loves Me

Our hopes for leaving the hospital disappeared the very next day.

The fluid behind Landen's lung was initially thought to be an infection. However, the lab results showed the fluid to be lymph, possibly caused by stress on his body.

The doctors ultimately diagnosed Landen with a chyle leak but were unsure of its origin, as it was not a common occurrence. Chyle leaks are typically the result of lymph node damage during heart surgery or, in rare cases, trauma resulting in death. Landen's situation was highly unusual.

The doctors informed us that we could not leave the hospital until they resolved the leak. Unfortunately, there was no way to stop it—we had to wait for it to heal. The timeframe for recovery was uncertain, ranging from weeks to possibly months. This was incredibly devastating, as it meant we couldn't be discharged to Gillette and had to endure this painful drain for an extended period.

To make it more comfortable, the doctors replaced the drain with a more permanent one, but the puncture in his side still appeared unpleasant.

Landen was moved back under the direction of the critical care doctor, resulting in increased medical attention. The doctors were perplexed and unsure how to proceed. They kept reiterating that they had never encountered a case like this and sought consultations with other doctors nationwide, hoping to find a solution.

One theory suggested fat was driving the chyle leak. As a result, the doctors put Landen on a strict IV nutrition regimen, with no solid food allowed.

The days became more difficult with the simple joy of solid food removed from Landen's routine. But an unexpected surprise came when Betsy reached out to me, asking if she could bring Will to the hospital to see Landen.

I agreed, but I asked her not to discuss what happened at the mall. Landen was still unaware of what had occurred, and we were not ready for him to know the truth. He wasn't mentally prepared to question why he was in the hospital, so I informed him that he had fallen and gotten seriously injured, and we were there for him to recover until his bones healed.

When Will and Landen reunited, they were overjoyed and spent their time playing games. Both had smiles on their faces throughout the visit.

However, after they left, Landen turned to me and asked, "Mommy, can we go home? I miss my friends."

Although my heart broke to have to tell him, I said, "I'm sorry, baby, but we can't go home yet. We have to stay until your bones are completely healed. Just a few more days."

His face fell, and I could see his exhaustion from the visit. Shortly after, he had an accident all over the bed, requiring a diaper and sheet change.

At that point, I decided that there would be no more visitors. It was too challenging for both Landen and me, as it was emotionally draining, and we had no idea when we could leave the hospital. Seeing people come and go, continuing their lives while we remained stuck, only made us feel more isolated. Therefore, I decided to limit visitors to only Dave and grandparents. I didn't want Landen to think about home because we could not go there.

MIRACLE AT THE MALL

That night, Landen didn't sleep. He tried to pull off the cast, the monitor wires, and the feeding tube out of his nose. He was done; he wanted to leave and go home so badly. It was an awful night, the worst so far.

Betsy had brought a picture of Landen, Will, and their friend Noah from preschool, which I initially hung up in the room. However, the following day, I took it down. It was heartbreaking to see Landen unable to do the things captured in that photo. He couldn't eat. He couldn't move freely due to the chyle leak tube. He could not play like he used to, or go home to see his friends. I didn't want him to feel the emotional pain of missing out on those experiences.

To protect Landen from seeing others do things he couldn't, I started skipping past any movie or TV scenes that showed people engaging in activities he couldn't do, like eating or bathing. When we Facetimed with Haden and Haley, I asked Dave not to show them eating breakfast or with wet hair, as it would only remind Landen of what he was missing out on.

I also stopped eating in his room. I made sure to have someone bring me a plate of food I could keep in the fridge, and I would discreetly eat when he was sleeping so he wouldn't see me or smell it on my breath. Once, he smelled a granola bar on my breath and desperately wanted a bite, so I learned my lesson and never did that again. We also made a rule for anyone entering his room: no food or drinks allowed.

As Haden and Haley started to miss me more, we planned for my parents to stay with Landen while Dave picked me up for a trip to a nearby bakery. It was my first time leaving the hospital, and it felt strange to be in a car. I told Landen I had to talk with the doctors so he wouldn't worry about where I was. Meanwhile, he had a great time, and when I returned, he was laughing and having so much fun. It was a much-needed distraction from our current reality for both of us.

Later that day, while Landen was napping, I noticed that he had put his blankie in his mouth, just like he used to do when he slept at home. I had wondered when this comforting habit would return, and it was a bittersweet reminder of those familiar routines.

While Landen slept, Courtney surprised us with a visit, bringing her kids, Owen and Evan. Since Landen was asleep, and I knew visitors were challenging for him, I met them downstairs and asked a nurse to keep an eye on Landen, asking him to let me know if Landen woke up.

Not long after I greeted Courtney and her children, a nurse let me know Landen was awake and asking for me.

Turning to Courtney, I said, "You can come up with me, but will you wait in the hallway and let me make sure he's okay?"

"Of course," she said, and we made our way back up to his room.

When I entered his room, he was crying and angry.

"I'm sorry I left, baby. Courtney is here with Owen and Evan, and everyone wants to see you," I said, leaning in to give him a hug.

Tearfully, he whispered, "I don't want them here because they'll see my diaper."

My heart breaking, I assured him, "We'll cover it up, so they'll never know. Let's just let them say hi really quick, and then they'll leave." He reluctantly agreed.

The visit was brief, and upon their departure, Landen was distraught.

We couldn't calm him down, so the nurse gave him some medicine to help calm him. That experience clarified that we could not have visitors, period. It was too much for Landen. He was still taking a lot of pain medicine. Nights were becoming challenging, as Landen needed me constantly. It felt like I had a newborn again, sleeping with one eye open.

However, on that particular night, Landen fell asleep while loudly singing "Jesus Loves Me" in his best voice. In the midst of all his pain and discomfort . . . dealing with delays and disappointing news . . . having to wear a diaper and feeling embarrassed . . . feeling trapped in a hospital bed, unable to run, play, or even see friends . . . there was Landen, singing "Jesus Loves Me" loudly for all to hear.

I made a note in my journal, reminding myself to shift my mindset back to gratitude. There were people in the world dealing with unimaginable horrors like mass shootings, car accidents, and kidnappings. These moms didn't get their children back. Yet here I was, sitting in Landen's bed, fortunate to have him with me, getting to hear him sing "Jesus Loves Me." That night, my gratitude rested on that thought.

> "We are pressed on every side by troubles, but we are not crushed. We are perplexed, but not driven to despair. We are hunted down, but never abandoned by God. We get knocked down, but we are not destroyed."
>
> — 2 Corinthians 4:8-9 NLT

> "Be thankful in all circumstances, for this is God's will for you who belong to Christ Jesus."
>
> — 1 Thessalonians 5:18 NLT

God, we're grateful for You! Thank You for all the times You have protected us and rescued us even when we were not aware. Thank You for the breath in our lungs. Thank You for life, freedom, and salvation. Thank You for sending Your Son, Jesus, into the world to die on a cross for our sins!

Chapter 24

Intense Pain

Landen's pain medications were taking a toll. His leg was still broken and in a spica cast, but it was almost fully healed. However, the lung drain was painful, so pain medications were necessary. Determining which medicine and how much was the main challenge.

He started screaming at night, frightened by a figure in the corner. The PICU doctors explained that it was hospital delirium, and assured me it was a common reaction after being hospitalized for so long. Still, I was scared.

That night, we had a new night nurse. Soon after she came in, she asked, "Could I pray for both of you?"

"Of course," I said. "Please."

It was a simple prayer. "God, let Your presence fill this room. Let there be no room for darkness in Your incredible light. In Jesus' name, amen."

Going to bed, I reflected on the belief that evil never wins. Although we had many fights ahead of us, we would not be defeated emotionally or physically. I knew we would have a unique, joy-filled life. We just had to keep pushing through.

Landen continued to experience occasional hallucinations, likely due to his medications. I had control over the medication he received.

When he was in pain, he could have morphine, which would make him feel good for an hour, but then he would crash and feel yucky. The question was always whether it was worth it to give him relief, knowing what would come afterward. I had to decide when to give him medication based on how much pain I felt he was in.

We were taking things day by day. Each day began with an X-ray at 5:00 am to check the fluid in his lungs. The plan was that if the chyle leak did not stop within 30 days, they would perform surgery to try to prevent it. We were waiting for the leak to stop naturally or for the 30-day mark to arrive for the surgery. The nurses then evaluated his eyes, blood pressure, lung sounds, and temperature. The trauma team would do the same and ask about his sleep and vomiting. The constant poking and prodding without much privacy was exhausting for both of us.

~

May 12th—Mother's Day—arrived, marking Day 30. The chyle leak, as well as the PIC line and blood thinners, were still present. Dave, Haden, and Haley came to the hospital to celebrate Mother's Day, and Dave surprised me with diamond earrings. But it was hard to focus on anything but the looming prospect of another surgery.

During their rounds, the doctors discussed not wanting to rush into surgery because they weren't sure if it would help. However, they ultimately decided to proceed.

I called our church and requested prayers for the leak to stop. The church family held a 24-hour prayer session. Lynne and her grandson Jamie came to the hospital to lay hands on Landen and pray for his healing. Jamie prayed boldly:

Dear Heavenly Father,
We come before You today to lift up little Landen in prayer. We stand together in faith, knowing that You are a God of miracles and endless love. Right now, we bind the enemy, and we reject any attack of the devil against this precious boy. Landen's life and health are in Your mighty hands, Lord.

We declare, with unwavering faith, that Landen's health will be completely restored, from the very tips of his toes to the top of his head. Every bone, every muscle, and every cell in his body will be renewed and healed by Your miraculous power."

At that point, Jamie began walking away. Then he suddenly stopped, came back and said this:

I see Landen running freely, jumping with joy, and playing in the sunlight, experiencing the fullness of life You have in store for him. Let him feel Your love and healing flow through every part of his being, Father.

We trust in You, Lord, and we thank You in advance for the restoration and joy that You are bringing into Landen's life. In Jesus' name, we pray. Amen.

We all joined in agreement with Jamie's prayer, and it was a powerful moment of faith and worship, as we all stood in awe, reflecting on God's healing power.

The surgery was scheduled for May 15th to stop the chyle leak. They planned to rough up the lung on the outside, intentionally causing scar tissue to form and hopefully stop the leak. Landen had to be intubated for the surgery. I made it clear to the doctors that if we proceeded, I needed him to come back to me extubated—I couldn't bear going through that whole process again.

During the surgery, I sat in silence with my mom, anxiously awaiting its completion. When the doctors finally reported that the surgery went well, I expected to see Landen emerge soon. However, it took longer than anticipated, and I grew worried. The PICU doctor approached me and explained that he was taking shallow breaths, which indicated significant pain. Landen needed to remain intubated until the pain subsided enough for deeper breaths. I was devastated and unprepared for this. I cried uncontrollably, feeling broken.

The day nurse, Heather, found me. She took hold of my shoulders.

"You are strong and capable. You can do this. The intubation is necessary for pain relief, but Landen will get through this."

I steeled myself, getting ahold of my emotions. "Thank you," I said. "You're right." I settled back down to wait for more news from the doctors.

One of the surgeons came and explained the extensive nature of the surgery and the pain Landen was experiencing.

"Why didn't anyone explain this to me beforehand?" I asked angrily. "No one told me he would be in this kind of pain!"

"I apologize, Mrs. Hoffmann. We should have gone through the details with you more thoroughly. I promise to walk through all these things together for future procedures."

The doctors initially wanted to move us to the critical care fishbowl hallway, but I adamantly refused because there was no shower in the room, and I hated leaving him. Eventually, they agreed to let us stay in the current room.

Landen was finally brought back to the room, still intubated. With God's strength, I mentally prepared myself to be with Landen while he remained intubated for the next few days.

The next day, Haden and Haley had a school program, and I agreed to attend even though I didn't want to leave the hospital. Dave and his mom stayed with Landen, reading books while he was intubated. I was shaking and had hives throughout the entire program, but despite my worries, I enjoyed watching Haden and Haley, who looked happy and did an excellent job. I knew they were well taken care of and that they were unaware of what was happening at the hospital.

Landen remained intubated for the next two days due to breathing problems.

While Landen was sedated, the doctors performed an ultrasound to check for the blood clot in his leg to ensure it hadn't grown or moved. However, the nurse informed me they couldn't find the blood clot. It was completely gone! The fact that the clot had resolved felt like a hug from God to help me through this intubation period.

During this time, Katie decided to come back and stay for a few days. The doctors informed me that the leak had partially moved from the lung to the belly, so a second drain needed to be installed because fluid was filling up his belly. Landen had to stay intubated for another day to give the doctors more time to figure out what was happening. This news was gut-wrenching. I wondered how I was going to sleep in his bed with tubes on each side of him.

During Landen's intubation period, I focused on being fearless. I had a lot of time to think and write. I was grateful for Katie's presence, as she supported me. I tried not to rely on my understanding but instead have a greater dependence on God.

> "The name of the LORD is a strong tower; the righteous run to it and are safe."
>
> — PROVERBS 18:10 NKJV

> "Consider it pure joy, my brothers and sisters, whenever you face trials of many kinds, because you know that the testing of your faith produces perseverance. Let perseverance finish its work so that you may be mature and complete, not lacking anything."
>
> — JAMES 1:2-4 NIV

Thank You, Lord, for working through our troubles and tribulations to show us how strong You are. Thank You for taking terrible situations and using them for our good. Thank You for using difficulties to produce perseverance, maturity, and character in us.

Chapter 25

The Man Who Did This

Sitting beside Landen's bed after a difficult night following his extubating, I received a message from my cousin Courtney informing me that the man responsible for Landen's suffering would be sentenced the next morning. She offered me the opportunity to write down anything I wanted to say to him. This is called a victim impact statement. I glanced at her message and set my phone aside.

I thought to myself, *No, I have nothing to say.*

However, later that night, with Landen tucked in bed, fast asleep and snoring, a firm conviction compelled me to write. So, I sat there next to him, using my phone as a flashlight, and wrote.

You may have intended to harm him, but God had a different plan! He intended it for good, to achieve what is happening now: the salvation of many lives.

On that day, you focused on yourself, your emotions, and your desire to harm someone else. I am saddened that you opted for anger and hatred. Something truly terrible must have happened to you for you to want to inflict this pain upon an innocent and sweet boy. I am sorry for what you have experienced. I hope God can change you and show you the true meaning of love someday...

I want you to understand that I forgive you, not because what you did was acceptable, not because I want to, but because God wants me to. You will not take any part of our family away from us. You will not steal our love, joy, or peace. I refuse to be filled with anger and hatred. I refuse to allow you to rob me of my happiness. My precious baby, my unique gift from God, will be alright because Jesus loves him deeply, just as He loves me.

He answered my prayers and returned Landen to me. You have taken nothing from us. On that day, you chose to listen to the devil. I do not have the authority to judge you or hate you. Instead, I am filled with God's love, overwhelming joy, and peace as I sit here in the hospital, witnessing my son heal in miraculous ways right before my eyes.

The world is witnessing how God works in this little boy I am fortunate enough to call my own. The devil tried to destroy him, but God saves. God always emerges victorious.

Someday, God will be the one to judge you, and I find peace in that. I surrender my burden to Him, and you will never occupy my thoughts again. I am finished with you.

God, take him.

Landen's Mom

After I shared what I had written with Courtney, her husband, Steve, mentioned to Dave that I had written something that would be read in court. Steve thought it would be a good idea for Dave to say something, but Dave had nothing to say and wanted nothing to do with it. Steve offered to write it for him, and Dave agreed.

Both statements were read to the man in custody on national TV, but I didn't watch the sentencing until almost a year later. The memories of writing that letter resurfaced, and I realized how far we had come.

As I watched, the man listened to both statements, standing with

MIRACLE AT THE MALL

his hands clasped behind his back as he slowly swayed and looked at the ground. It seemed to me like he couldn't care less. He stepped forward and said, "No" into the microphone when asked if he wanted to respond. That was it.

While I have no intention of pursuing a relationship with this man, I am genuinely curious about where he will go in life. The fact that he had intentions to harm a 5-year-old boy is unquestionably heartbreaking, and I yearn to see if God can positively change his life.

My desire is not for him to feel guilt or regret but to find a new purpose. Can someone like him, who has never experienced God's love and led a life detached from Jesus, undergo a profound transformation and have the emptiness in his heart filled with the love of Jesus? The answer is yes, he can—but he has to make the choice to receive Jesus Christ as his Lord and Savior.

I have been praying for God to reveal Himself and convict this man of his sin, bringing him to his knees to acknowledge his wrongdoing. I want him to understand that he is one of God's children, even though he is one of God's lost children as far as anyone knows right now.

If this man were to receive Jesus as Lord and let God turn his life around, it would be a powerful testament to the world about God's love. It's not about my personal feelings but rather the opportunity to show him that God's love surpasses everything else and that only God can fill the void he feels in his life. If he chooses to reject Jesus Christ and thus spend eternity in hell, that is his decision, but he does not have to choose that. No one has to choose that.

God has given everyone a "get out of Hell free" card through the cross of Jesus Christ. All we have to do is turn to Him, acknowledge that we have sinned, ask for His forgiveness, and give our lives to Him. I was also a sinner in need of a Savior before I turned away from sin, asked for forgiveness, and gave my life to Jesus Christ. That doesn't mean I'm perfect now, but it means that my life belongs to Jesus, and I do my best to obey Him and live the life He wants me to live.

Someday, I hope to hear that the man who did this has received Jesus as his Lord and Savior and become a new creation in Christ.

"For all have sinned and fall short of the glory of God"

— Romans 3:23 ESV

"For the wages of sin is death, but the free gift of God is eternal life in Christ Jesus our Lord."

— Romans 6:23 ESV

But what does it say? "The word is near you; it is in your mouth and in your heart," that is, the message concerning faith that we proclaim: If you declare with your mouth, "Jesus is Lord," and believe in your heart that God raised him from the dead, you will be saved. For it is with your heart that you believe and are justified, and it is with your mouth that you profess your faith and are saved."

— Romans 10:8-10 NIV

If you don't have a personal relationship with Jesus as Savior and Lord of your life, you can change that right now. All you have to do is give your life to Him. Just pray the prayer below and mean it in your heart.

Thank You, Jesus, for dying on our cross for my sins. I confess with my mouth that I have sinned and fallen short of the glory of God. I ask for forgiveness for my sins, and I give my life to You, Jesus.

Chapter 26

The Power of Hope

It had been 46 days since Landen was admitted to the hospital, and I was filling out my third journal. With much enthusiasm, I inscribed on the opening page, "THIS JOURNAL WILL LEAD US BACK HOME!" This was my outlet for maintaining a positive mindset and manifesting the necessary miracles, especially as Landen's chyle leak prevented us from going home.

The leak was becoming more and more frustrating. I found myself praying and believing even harder for answers. I was willing to do anything to make this leak stop.

Later that night, I spoke with my cousin Brian, who found some case studies about children with chyle leaks. Interestingly, they mainly focused on children who'd had heart surgery, but Landen's case was different, where the leak persisted even with IV nutrition. He informed me that Dr. Wahoff and a new addition to our medical team, Dr. Singewald, an interventional radiologist, would be coming to discuss a new plan.

They soon stopped by, and their new plan involved performing an ink study on Landen. Dr. Singewald would inject ink into Landen's veins and observe if and where any leakage occurred. This would allow them to identify the exact source of the leak instead of relying on guesswork. Then they could formulate a more targeted approach to repairing the leak. I wanted a better solution. To me, this felt like another procedure without a guarantee of resolving the issue. However, it was our best option, so I agreed.

Before Dr. Wahoff departed, he shared a story. "There's a mother I encountered a few years ago whose son also experienced a chyle leak. If anyone knows what you're going through, it's her. You should consider reaching out to her. Maybe she can help ease your mind or give you a mother's perspective."

He gave me a piece of paper with her name and phone number. "I understand that initiating contact with someone new can be daunting, particularly during such challenging circumstances. However, connecting with individuals who have undergone similar experiences can offer emotional support and valuable insights. When you feel ready, or if you ever do, I can assist you in taking the first step in reaching out to her."

I thanked him for the advice and tucked the paper into my Bible.

As we headed to bed that night, a newfound hope filled our hearts for the approaching day. We eagerly anticipated an X-ray of Landen's broken femur, hoping to determine if it had fully healed, which would allow us to remove that cumbersome spica cast. The possibility of this thrilled us because during brief breaks from the cast, Landen amazed us by lifting his leg way over his head, causing us to laugh. We couldn't help but marvel at his newfound flexibility.

Whatever situations we face in life, it's so important to maintain hope. Without hope, we can start to sink into a downward spiral. But when we have Jesus, there is always hope. Hope for change. Hope for healing. Hope for a future that is better than our present reality.

As we drifted off to sleep that night, our hopes were fixed on the possibility of saying goodbye to the cast and receiving a date for the ink study that would bring us one step closer to going home. This optimism and anticipation comforted us as dreams gently carried us away.

"We have this hope as an anchor for the soul, firm and secure. It enters the inner sanctuary behind the curtain, where our forerunner, Jesus, has entered on our behalf"

— Hebrews 6:19-20 NIV

"May the God of hope fill you with all joy and peace in believing, so that by the power of the Holy Spirit you may abound in hope"

— Romans 15:13 ESV

God, we know You have our lives in Your hands. Please fill us with joy, peace, and hope as we put our trust in You.

Chapter 27

Finding Strength

The morning of Landen's X-ray was supposed to be exciting. Going there and getting some fun stickers from the technician was always an adventure. Little did we know that this particular visit would bring unexpected news.

Dr. Engels, the bone doctor, was on vacation, but his team sent the X-ray images to him for review. My mom and I were in the room, playing games with Landen, when we were told it was time for physical therapy. We ventured downstairs, enjoying the chance to leave our room for the second time that day. However, while we were at therapy, we suddenly got a call to return to our room immediately for urgent news about Landen's leg. The atmosphere was tense, and I couldn't help but feel uneasy.

As we entered our room, a member of the orthopedics team was waiting for us with the X-ray images displayed on a computer. She broke the devastating news: Landen's femur had shifted and re-broken. It happened when he was learning to stand and bear weight.

The realization hit me like a ton of bricks.

I could see the broken bone on the X-ray, and I couldn't comprehend how they missed it. I felt anger and frustration building up inside me. No wonder he could lift his leg so high; it was broken, and the pain medications had masked it. I couldn't understand how this had happened, and the weight of it all left me broken and defeated. All I wanted was for everyone to go so I could be alone with Landen. I needed time to process this heartbreaking news.

In addition, we were informed that Landen would need surgery in the morning to reset the bones and get a new cast. It would be more permanent this time since he was awake and moving around. During this surgery he would have to be intubated again, but the doctors reassured me extubating wouldn't be a problem because they wouldn't be touching his lungs, just focusing on his leg.

In hindsight, I believe Landen's second break was God's way of making sure Landen stayed in bed and wasn't up walking around while they figured out why the chyle leak wouldn't stop.

I had to decide between an entire leg cast up to his waist or an external fixator device. Landen couldn't bear weight on his legs, so a regular cast would make diaper changes challenging for the next six to eight weeks. It would also be uncomfortable and difficult to clean. I couldn't even bear the thought of it, so I chose the external fixator, which involved three screws going directly into his bone through the skin. Despite having to deal with three additional wounds on his leg, this option would allow him more mobility and easier diaper changes. Neither choice was ideal, but I had to choose the one that seemed best for Landen.

With our decision made, we prepared ourselves for surgery. I didn't want a crowd in the waiting room with us this time. It wasn't a celebration—this was a battle. As I sat there, feeling defeated and overwhelmed, I prayed for strength and for the surgery to be over quickly.

Another six to eight weeks in bed, in a diaper, felt like a massive setback when we were so close to Landen being able to walk around. I couldn't help but feel a sense of despair.

After the surgery, as we settled back into our room, Landen was dizzy and scared to move his leg.

"I know it looks strange, but this will help you heal super-fast.

Soon, you'll be running, jumping, and playing! I promise it will be worth the wait," I told Landen, encouraging him to gently move his leg to get used to the feeling.

We were now waiting for news about the ink study, eager to know when it would occur. The devil constantly tried to throw challenges our way, but I was determined to maintain my peace and joy, ensuring Landen remained oblivious to our difficulties. To him, all that mattered was patiently waiting for his bones to heal while talking to friends, visiting the toy store, and diligently working on therapies.

So, we settled in again, fully aware that leaving the hospital wouldn't happen soon. We'd been taking care of his teeth by using an oral sponge with toothpaste built-in, then rinsing with water and spitting into a suction straw or a bowl since he couldn't get up to use the bathroom. But I came up with an idea—I would go to Target and buy some new toys, fun pajamas, a toothbrush, and toothpaste. He'd been stuck in hospital clothes and gowns due to wires and various obstacles, but I'd had enough of that. I wanted him to feel more normal, so I was determined to make some changes.

When Dave came later that day, I asked him to stay with Landen while my parents took me to Target. It was time to break free from the monotonous hospital routine and embrace some normalcy.

Before I left, I was informed they were putting the ink study on hold due to the decreased fluid output. When we are going through the major trials of our lives, there comes a point where we get extremely tired. We get weary and we feel like we can't go on. But it's in those moments when God's strength is perfected through our weakness. When we are weak, we just have to keep going back to Him, humbling ourselves, and asking for Him to supply His strength.

The amazing thing is, He will do it!

One day, around this time, I was in the hospital room shower while Landen was gone for a procedure. There was no one else in the room. But when I stepped out, I noticed a cleaning lady mopping our floor. She was singing "Jesus Loves Me" so beautifully, her voice filling the room as she danced with the mop.

It was such a beautiful moment, another reminder of God's

presence every step of the way. She didn't know us and I didn't know her. I only saw her that day and I never saw her again. God gives us those little winks and nudges to strengthen us and keep us going.

We need those, because trials often continue on way past the many times we think they're going to end. Sometimes it feels like the trial will never end. In those times, we have to ask for His strength because our own strength will run out.

Once you've asked for His strength and you've gotten it—remember that the God we serve is a Way-Maker. He'll make a way to get it done, fix it, shift it, or turn it. Even when there doesn't seem to be a way, agree with God that you will serve Him, maintain faith in Him, and wait on Him. His blessings are always worth the wait and always right on time.

During this time, God was teaching me to have patience without grumbling, and I was trying my best to follow that lesson. I was learning to find joy without looking too far ahead or dwelling on the past. Enjoying each day was my primary focus.

With summer approaching, school would be ending soon for Haden and Haley. I couldn't wait for us to return home together, but I understood that the time wasn't right yet. We would figure out a plan when the time came.

> "Let us not become weary in doing good, for at the proper time we will reap a harvest if we do not give up"
>
> — GALATIANS 6:9 NIV

> "I have heard your prayer and seen your tears; I will heal you."
>
> — 2 KINGS 20:5 NIV

God, please be with the person who is reading this right now and struggling through a trial. Let Your peace wash over them. Let your strength and peace fill them to overflowing. Give them time alone with

You in worship, so that you can refill their tank, and reset their emotions. Fill them with joy, and when the time is right, give them their breakthrough and bring their suffering to an end. Thank You, Jesus!

Chapter 28

Outlasting the Enemy

The enemy was trying to wear me down and fill me with doubt. I refused to let him succeed. I knew that when I couldn't take it anymore, God would step in and reveal something I'd never seen. I had faith that He would rescue us.

I found myself constantly marveling at the incredible design of our bodies and how God made us to heal. Landen's body was trying its best to recover, but something was hindering it, something we still needed to uncover. So, I continued to rebuke attacks from the devil and remain patient, waiting for the moment when we finally found what we needed to help his body heal.

Spiritual warfare is a lot like boxing, long distance running, or other athletic contests that require extreme endurance. Often, if you can simply outlast your opponent, you can emerge victorious.

So I was determined to do that. But you don't do that by focusing on your opponent. Instead, you rebuke. You trample. You cast down. And you keep your focus on God and His promises. The promises of God are like fuel. Just like a marathon runner needs Gatorade, we need the Word of God to keep us going during these times.

I began to focus on the fact that God has a reason for everything He does, and for everything He allows to happen. That meant the delay was for a reason, and if I could maintain a positive attitude and try to embrace whatever lesson God wanted to teach me during this waiting period, the reason would be revealed to us.

A page from the photo scrapbook I made

I was confident His favor was upon us, and we could feel the world's prayers lifting us. We were eternally grateful for prayers from our loved ones and even strangers. There was no more excellent gift than prayer and intercession on our behalf.

Finally, the doctors were ready to conduct an MRI to locate the leak causing the fluid buildup in Landen's belly. They would then use a tiny needle to inject sticky ink through his veins, similar to poppy seed oil, to seal the leak. They expressed confidence in this method, even though it was new and experimental. However, I was uncertain about the idea because once the ink was in his veins, it would stay there forever, leaving a reminder during future X-rays. The doctors assured me it wouldn't harm him, but we had to always be aware. Despite my hesitation, I desperately wanted this leak to be gone, so I trusted the doctors and moved forward with the experimental procedure.

While we waited for his MRI to finish, I noticed an empty room with a different view down the hall. It faced in the opposite direction of ours, and I saw that the bathroom was located around the corner instead of within the living space. I requested that we be moved there to have a fresh view from our window when Landen returned from the ink study. I also planned to remove some things from our walls, as if we were preparing to move out instead of moving in. By making these changes, I wanted to shift our minds and focus on moving forward rather than feeling stuck where we were.

Following Landen's MRI, we went to the heart wing of the hospital, where they would perform the procedure to seal the leak. Dave and my parents were with me, sitting together in the waiting room and offering prayers.

While we waited, I received a text from our church family, informing me they had a room full of people fasting and praying for us. They also sent a video of a song written for Landen by someone from the church. I handed one earbud to Dave, and together, we sat in the waiting room with tears streaming down our faces, listening to this powerful song. I could feel the presence of God in that room.

When the doctors finished, they came out to speak with us. They expressed robust hopefulness.

Dave asked, "On a scale of 1 to 10, how confident are you that you found and sealed the leak?"

Dr. Singewald hesitated to provide a definitive answer, not wanting to give false hope, as this was new and untested. He said, "I gave it my best shot. I saw the leak and sprayed the entire area with the sticky ink, hopefully sealing it."

We left the conversation feeling good but not entirely relieved. Everything remained uncertain, and it was yet another wait-and-see situation.

While Landen was intubated, the doctors drained two liters of fluid from his belly. He felt so much better with all that built-up pressure gone. However, it didn't take long for the pressure to build back up. His tummy kept getting bigger, and he was constantly throwing up.

Dr. Wahoff came back to examine Landen. He said, "It looks like the chest tube was sealed, but the leak has returned in Landen's belly. Now that I have a target, I want to try more ink."

Exhausted and anxious, I said, "Go ahead." But it took hours for anyone to come.

I wanted to get it over with. All I could think about was poor Landen, getting sedated and poked and prodded too much. I was sick of it. No one had answers. It was all guesswork.

Dr. Wahoff mentioned that this might be the right time to reach out to the other boy's mom for support in making it through the chyle leak. I knew it had to stop at some point, but *when?* Maybe she would help me understand that it sucks while you're in it, but it will end one day. That's all I wanted to know—that it would stop one day. If I understood that, I could wait and be patient.

It was now two months from the day Landen was thrown: June 12th, 2019. We'd been in the hospital for 62 days. I wanted him to be happy, playing, and smiling again. He'd been so sick and weak for too long.

"For though I fall, I will rise again. Though I sit in darkness, the LORD will be my light."

— Micah 7:8 NLT

"In his kindness God called you to share in his eternal glory by means of Christ Jesus. So after you have suffered a little while, he will restore, support, and strengthen you, and he will place you on a firm foundation"

— 1 Peter 5:10 NLT

Thank You, Lord, for Your many promises. We know that Your Word has power and will accomplish the purpose for which You send it. We stand on Your promises in faith, and declare that we will come out of this and we will see the complete and total victory through Jesus!

Chapter 29

Tapping Out

Dave came to wait with me for the next attempt to seal the leak.

Landen enjoyed tasting beverages since he couldn't have food, so the morning was challenging as we waited for the ink study. Knowing he'd be sedated again. Knowing he couldn't have any drinks before surgery. It broke my heart to see how difficult this was for him. Thankfully, Dave brought Landen a toy, like he usually did before or after surgeries and procedures. Landen didn't want to go through most of them, so the gift usually brought him a bit of joy and served as a temporary distraction.

I pleaded with God. *Lord, fill the surgery room with Your presence. Guide the doctor's hand to locate the exact leak spot and seal it once and for all.*

When it was time to take Landen away, I couldn't go with them. They gave him sleeping medicine while he was with me, so I gave him a kiss and let them take him. I sat alone in his room, waiting anxiously for Landen to return, while Dave paced in the hallway, seeking reassurance from the doctors he encountered. I prayed fervently, asking God to seal the leak in the name of Jesus.

Deciding now was a good time, I mustered the courage to call the mom of the other child who had experienced a chyle leak.

She answered immediately, greeting me in a warm tone after I introduced myself. "Hi, it's so nice to hear from you. I've been waiting for you to call."

Her warmth and willingness to talk soothed me, and it was a relief to connect with someone who understood what we were going through.

I asked her about her son's leak, and she said, "The chyle leak continued for several days before it stopped suddenly. Maybe it will be the same with your son's leak, and it will just end one day all of a sudden."

I was grateful for her words, yet cautious since I knew Landen's situation was different and more complex than that of her son. Nonetheless, her willingness to take my call and provide hope was incredibly kind.

I asked, "What is your son's current care routine now that the leak has been resolved?"

"There are only occasional check-ups to monitor the situation. He's been doing really well. I hope it is the same for your son." Although this information brought relief, I couldn't entirely rely on it as an indicator for our situation due to the unique nature of Landen's case. I thanked her and said goodbye.

When Landen finally returned, he was completely spent. The surgeons were hopeful again and told me they gave it their best shot at sealing this leak. I had to trust what they said, but in the depths of my soul, I whispered to God, "I need you. Please help us, God. I can't do this anymore."

Tears streamed down my face, and I felt utterly drained emotionally. It was nighttime, so we tried to go to bed, but Landen's discomfort was undeniable. His chest was filled with residue from being intubated again, but he was too weak to cough it up, so we had no choice but to leave it be. His belly looked so painful, and we kept his pain under control throughout the night so that he could get some much-needed sleep.

I was shaken to my core. It was unbearable to witness him in so much pain without any answers. I closed my eyes and tried to sleep.

The following day, we woke up and checked Landen's drain. He produced even more fluid than before. I couldn't believe it—it felt like we were being pushed to our limits, worn down by relentless challenges. In my journal, I wrote that the devil couldn't take Landen out, so instead, he was attempting to wear us out.

I was reaching my breaking point.

Landen was in excruciating pain, taking shallow breaths. They put him back on oxygen to help him breathe more comfortably. He stopped talking altogether; every word had become too painful. The dressing on his drain was leaking and soaked. They had no choice but to change it, and he was too exhausted to fight.

I didn't want anyone to come to our room anymore, not even my parents. It was too uncomfortable to sit and keep explaining what was happening because none of us had any clue. My mom said she had to come, even if it was just to sit down the hall, so they did.

The hole in his side from the drain stretched so much that it was causing fluid to leak all over the bed. They informed us they'd have to sedate him and stitch it up.

When I needed strength the most, God surrounded us with our favorite nurses and doctors. We had Paige and Katrin, who were with us from the beginning. There was also Mary Ann, another one of Landen's favorite night nurses, and even Dr. Ekinberry, whom we hadn't seen in weeks. Their presence gave me a renewed sense of fight in my spirit, and I was ready to battle alongside this fantastic team.

With Katrin as our night nurse, we were relieved to get some real rest. However, at 5:00 am, Landen started grunting and struggling to breathe. Two PICU surgeons, Dr. Wahoff and Dr. Jenkins (not his real name), were called in. After taking an X-ray, they discovered that he had fluid on his left side, and they needed to immediately place a second drain.

Walking into the hallway with Katrin while they placed the drain, I said, "We can't go back to having two drains. It's just too much. How much pain can his little body go through?"

She hugged me and reassured me that Landen was strong, and they were doing everything they could.

I returned to the room to find him alert and breathing better. The new drain had already drained two liters of fluid, relieving the pressure on his lungs and allowing him to breathe more easily. Despite my dislike for the drain, I felt grateful since it meant he was getting the necessary oxygen.

Later that day, Dave and the twins planned to visit. It was close to dinner time, so we thought I could take the twins out while Dave stayed with Landen. However, I noticed a big kink in the drain, which made me suspect another fibrin blockage. I informed the nurses, who paged Dr. Jenkins.

When he arrived, he believed the drain was clogged and asked me to wear a mask while he worked on unclogging it and changing the dressing. As scared as I was, I couldn't leave Landen's side. I couldn't bear to watch the procedure, so I looked away. Holding Landen's hand, I focused on his face, knowing he was unaware due to the sedation drugs.

Dr. Jenkins was puzzled by the green fluid coming out of the tube instead of the usual yellow color. He called for help and requested an X-ray team to examine the situation. Everything was happening rapidly, with a sense of emergency in the air. The X-ray revealed that the drain had punctured Landen's stomach, causing the green fluid, which was identified as stomach bile, to leak out. Dr. Jenkins explained that Landen needed immediate emergency surgery to fix this puncture. I was in shock. The accident had taken place right in front of me. It was the worst outcome I could have imagined—another surgery due to a mistake.

I sent a mass text about the situation to our families and loved ones. Everyone rushed to the hospital while Landen was in surgery, feeling a mix of fear and urgency.

I clung to Psalm 73:26 (NIV), "My flesh and my heart may fail, but God is the strength of the heart and my portion forever."

Help me, God, I pleaded over and over.

When Dave arrived, he was furious about what had happened and overwhelmed by the crowd in our room. We both desired solitude to process the overwhelming emotions we were experiencing. Our loved ones respectfully left and sat silently in the waiting room. It was undoubtedly the worst night we had faced in our entire lives.

The rapidity with which everything unfolded and how quickly Landen was taken down to the basement for emergency surgery constantly replayed in my mind. I felt like everything was spiraling out of control, leaving me lost, sad, and completely shattered. As I sobbed, waiting for Landen to come out of surgery, all I could pray was, "God, give Landen back to us."

Dave called Brian to clarify the situation. Brian quickly arrived and attempted to provide answers, but we had to wait for the surgeons to finish and come out before receiving a complete understanding. Fortunately, the surgery was not lengthy, but it was disheartening to know that Landen's stomach had to be cut open for the third time due to this unfortunate accident.

Dr. Wahoff explained they initially suspected the puncture had occurred in Landen's intestine, which could have been fatal as the fluid from the intestine cannot enter the bloodstream. The fact that it was his stomach potentially saved his life, but the need for another painful surgery due to an accident broke my heart. I couldn't help but wonder how much more his body could endure.

As I entered the recovery room, my heart shattered at the sight of him, my precious child. His abdomen was covered in wounds, cuts, and pokes. It was the worst pain I had ever seen him endure, and it overwhelmed me to the point that I felt like I couldn't breathe. My family sat at the end of the hall, but I couldn't bring myself to face them and share the details of what had happened. I didn't want hugs or sympathy. I just wished for the night to end.

Katrin, our night nurse, gave me a sense of security. She was amazing at caring for Landen all night after the surgery. Given the two drains coming out of his body and the recent surgery, Katrin wanted unrestricted access to care for him from every angle, so she kindly asked me to sleep on the couch. Throughout that night, Landen was slightly aware and would request ice chips. Katrin lovingly fed the ice chips to him while she sat by his side, diligently tending to his pain and wounds. Meanwhile, worn out and defeated, I succumbed to sleep on the couch, aided by Benadryl, desperately needing rest.

Katrin became a lifeline for us that night. During such challenging moments, it was truly unique to realize how much we appreciated the healthcare professionals there with us, supporting and caring for us in many ways.

Sometimes, we just have to tap out and let another person help us through our trials—even if only for a single day or a few brief hours. We have to be able to rest and recharge, and sometimes the only way to do that is to lean on others. I was thankful for Katrin stepping up the way she did.

Once we rest and regain clarity, we must lift ourselves from the floor and proceed with whatever lies ahead. We have fought, we have struggled, and we have taken a rest. But what will tomorrow bring?

Our resolve must remain strong. We must face what's next. We will make it to the end of the trial.

> "Therefore put on the full armor of God, so that when the day of evil comes, you may be able to stand your ground, and after you have done everything, to stand"
>
> — Ephesians 6:13 NIV

Lord, I pray for anyone reading this who is on the front lines and has no strength left, that You would send them reinforcements. Let them rest, recharge, and find the resolve to keep fighting another day. Thank You, Lord, that You will see them through to the end of this trial, in Jesus name, amen.

Chapter 30

Breakthrough

I felt trapped.

Our world revolved around a tiny room. Occasionally, we would go for a walk or a small adventure, but then we were reconnected to various machines and drains, making every movement slow and calculated. I could only eat and shower when Landen was sleeping, so I had to be quick about it.

He was still struggling to breathe, and the doctors informed me that besides the lymph fluid issue, the stress his body endured from multiple surgeries was also causing more fluid buildup. His entire body was puffy and swollen, making it hard to recognize him.

As usual, 5:00 am meant it was time for an X-ray to monitor the fluid. They told me it looked a bit better, most likely due to the two drains helping Landen breathe. However, as much as these drains were helping in the short term, they were temporary solutions. The real issue was the ongoing leak that no one could figure out.

There was an infection around the IV in his hand from surgery, which worried Katrin. She told me that to prevent it from worsening, they had to give Landen four shots. I couldn't believe it—shots, something he hated, like all kids. It felt like we were torturing him, and

I couldn't help but wonder how much more pain he'd have to endure. When it came time for the shots, Katrin and three other nurses held Landen down, and I held him in the bed while tears streamed down my face as he cried out in pain.

Instead of moving toward healing, it felt like Landen's condition kept getting worse. He had two chest tubes, a long incision on his belly that needed daily dressing, a broken leg, and puncture wounds all over his fragile body. I desperately longed for answers, praying for God to intervene. I wrote in my journal, pouring out my heart and begging God for a significant breakthrough.

After Landen fell asleep that night, a doctor approached me and said, "You know you can't maintain this warrior status forever, right?"

In that moment, determination welled up inside me like never before. I couldn't believe what he said, and I looked him straight in the eye and responded, "Watch me."

In the morning, I spoke with Dr. Wahoff about returning to a fat-free diet, similar to when the chyle leak started, as the IV nutrition didn't seem to be making any difference. This would allow Landen to feel more normal and take a few bites of food. They agreed, and we excitedly discussed it throughout the day.

When the time came to eat, we were cautioned to take it easy. We ordered a fruit cup and some rice. Landen managed to have a few bites of fruit and a small amount of rice, but his medication made him feel full quickly.

However, the next time Landen tried to eat, he immediately threw up. Throughout the day, he continued to throw up and have diarrhea. Our new doctor, Dr. Linden, approached me to discuss the possibility of a new issue in Landen's belly and expressed deep concern about the vomiting. He believed Landen had an infection and suggested a CT scan to see if there were any visible problems.

Despite the vomiting and diarrhea, we tried to let Landen enjoy tiny sips of his buffet of drinks—the bright spot in his days. However, Dr. Linden expressed concern about the continuous vomiting, suggesting that we may have to stop the drinks. I pleaded with him not to take away our drinks, and thankfully, he left for the night after our discussion. I called Dave and asked him to text Dr. Wahoff, urging him to tell Dr. Linden to let us keep our drinks. Dave sent the text immediately.

Throughout the night Landen vomited. I couldn't take it anymore—it was all day and now all night. Watching my poor baby in so much pain was gut-wrenching.

The following morning, I contacted Dave again, urging him to call Dr. Wahoff and stress the urgent need for a CT scan. Landen's incessant vomiting was becoming increasingly concerning, and I felt that we couldn't wait any longer. It was Friday, and waiting the entire weekend without answers felt unbearable.

Dr. Linden returned in the morning and agreed to order the CT scan. Once Landen went for the scan, we anxiously waited for the results. Finally, Dr. Linden came to our room, but instead of delivering the news, he sat at the nurses' station with sparkling water in hand and a knowing smile. We were still waiting for Dave to arrive. Seeing Dr. Linden act so calmly frustrated me, as if he held the answers but refused to share them until everyone was present.

I felt overwhelmed and on the verge of a breakdown. It seemed like I might lose Landen, and the stress put me in fight-or-flight mode. Dr. Linden's smirk and casual behavior intensified my feelings. I wished I could remove him from the situation and rely on Dr. Wahoff, the doctor I trusted because of his connection with Brian and his being with us since day one.

Once Dave arrived, he could see how angry and close to my breaking point I was. Dave approached Dr. Linden and suggested they discuss Landen's situation outside, trying to shield me from further distress. However, Dr. Linden refused, insisting everyone needed to hear the news.

He revealed that the results of the CT scan showed a kinked small bowel. He explained the need to insert a tube through Landen's nose and stomach to address the issue, providing his intestines with a much-needed break. He emphasized that nothing, whether spit, stomach bile, or anything else, should enter his intestine. It all had to bypass, hence the need for the tube. He reassured us that after a few days of rest, Landen could resume drinking.

I couldn't believe it. Landen was already burdened with so many tubes in his nose, and they wanted to add another one. I was infuriated that Dr. Linden seemed to deliver this news as if it were a happy solution. He didn't acknowledge the underlying problem: the leak.

Overwhelmed by emotions, I walked out of the room, tears streaming down my face, and ran down near the windows at the end of the hallway. Though I had nowhere else to run, I couldn't bear to stay and listen to anything else Dr. Linden had to say. I just wanted to escape. Thankfully, my mom and Dave remained in the room, listening to Dr. Linden.

Soon after, Noel, one of Dr. Linden's nurses, found me. "You need to hear what Dr. Linden has to say."

I resisted, curled up in a ball, and told her, "I can't handle any more information." I felt like everything was spiraling—they had taken away the drinks, and Landen was in immense pain. My fight seemed to fade away.

Noel firmly grasped my shoulder, looking directly into my eyes, and said, "Kari, he found the answer to the leak. This is going to be over."

Stunned, I stopped crying, wiped my nose, and looked at her. "What?" I uttered, unable to comprehend what she was saying.

Noel explained that Dr. Linden had been concerned about the distinct dark blue veins he observed all over Landen's chest throughout the week. He knew this wasn't normal, along with his struggle to breathe. Dr. Linden had discussed the possibility of doing a vein study or exploring the possibility of an infection in his stomach from the previous surgery. He recognized that something was seriously wrong. Noel assured me that Dr. Linden had tirelessly searched for answers, delving into research and considering various possibilities until he found the cause.

As I stood there, trying to process the shocking revelation that Dr.

Miracle at the Mall

Linden had discovered the reason behind the persistent leak, my mom came running down the hall. She urgently told me they had seen the root cause. The CT scan had revealed a severe restriction in Landen's vena cava, the central vein leading to his heart. This explained why the leak wouldn't stop; his body was under such strain trying to repair the damage to his heart and ensure blood flow.

Dr. Linden had already contacted the heart team, who had left for the weekend, and asked them to return immediately to place a stent in Landen's vein that night. The goal was to open up the vein and restore proper blood flow. This newfound understanding provided hope, as resolving the pressure on his body should allow him to heal.

Despite still being in a state of shock, I hurried back to the room, my mind racing with thoughts of the upcoming surgery. Time was of the essence, and I couldn't bear the thought of waiting any longer. Everyone was called to gather. My mom reached out to our loved ones, urging them to come to the hospital and join us in prayer during this critical procedure.

The heart team arrived and spoke to us, assuring us they would do everything possible to place the stent and open Landen's vein, without making any explicit promises.

We sat in Landen's empty room, a heavy silence enveloping the air as we bowed our heads in prayer. It felt different from any other prayer I had experienced during this time. Instead of overwhelming worry, a sense of hope and excitement washed over me. It was as if God had given me back my peace. Instead of defeat and despair, I felt a true sense of relief.

Dave called Brian, and he arrived promptly. The two of them walked the hallway together, discussing the potential outcomes of the surgery. However, this time, everyone's demeanor brimmed with quiet optimism. It seemed like we were on the cusp of finally ending this ordeal.

When the surgery was complete, we received the call that Landen had been moved to the recovery room. This was the moment of truth we had been waiting for. We were ready.

Kari Hoffmann

In a hushed whisper, I prayed, "Jesus, prepare my heart for what lies ahead. Let Your presence and strength wash over me."

"The Lord will fight for you; you need only to be still."

— Exodus 14:14 NIV

Chapter 31

A Hidden Miracle

As the cardiac team entered the room, I couldn't help but feel an overwhelming sense of gratitude for these surgeons. They were new to us, as we had not yet required their care during Landen's time at the hospital.

Dr. Rios and Dr. Vezmar greeted us with beaming smiles, eager to share their success. Standing in a circle, they explained that Landen's vena cava had torn 98% during the initial injury. The vena cava only remained intact because the inflammation caused by trauma and his being intubated in bed for 11 days provided enough stability for the body to reattach it gradually. Due to the intense inflammation in his body, this injury had remained hidden. Dr. Rios also informed us that injuring the vena cava typically results in immediate death, so it wasn't on anyone's radar to look for such an injury.

The fact that Landen survived this particular injury was another jaw-dropping, medical-science-defying miracle from our great God!

In its fantastic resilience, and undoubtedly guided by God's own hand, Landen's body had formed new pathways to ensure blood flow to his heart as the vena cava healed. This explained the prominence of veins in his chest. The surgeons had successfully placed a 10mm stent, which was usually adult-sized, into Landen's heart without any complications—another miracle hug from God.

This stent opened up Landen's central vein, allowing blood to flow freely once again and relieving the immense stress his body had endured in getting blood to his heart. The relief in the room was palpable. Finally, they had resolved the main issue. *Thank you, Jesus*! I prayed.

I couldn't wait to be reunited with Landen, this time with a sense of relief rather than uncertainty. It was truly incredible to think that we had to witness fluid pouring out of him before realizing the severity of his heart condition. Without Dr. Linden's fresh eyes and innovative thinking, I don't know if anyone could have unraveled this mystery.

I am very grateful for Dr. Linden.

Later that evening, after everyone had left and I found myself alone with Landen, I gazed out the window at the breathtaking Minneapolis skyline, brilliantly illuminated under the night sky. Suddenly, Dr. Linden entered the room. Overwhelmed by emotions, tears streamed down my face as I embraced him.

He returned my hug and said, "This challenging journey—with all the warning signs, obstacles, and painful moments—was necessary to find a resolution. It is my deepest desire to witness Landen grow up and embrace the role of a wise old grandfather, bouncing his grandchildren on his knee."

"I want that, too," I told him with a smile.

As the mystery of Landen's chyle leak was solved, other steps in his healing journey began to make sense. Although rebreaking his leg was devasting at the time, his restricted movement was actually a blessing because, had he been up and walking with such an obstructed vein, the consequences could have been dire. It turns out God allowed the leg to remain broken, providing the doctors with the necessary time to diagnose the issue with his heart.

The phrase "God works in mysterious ways" had never been more real and personal to me than at that moment.

MIRACLE AT THE MALL

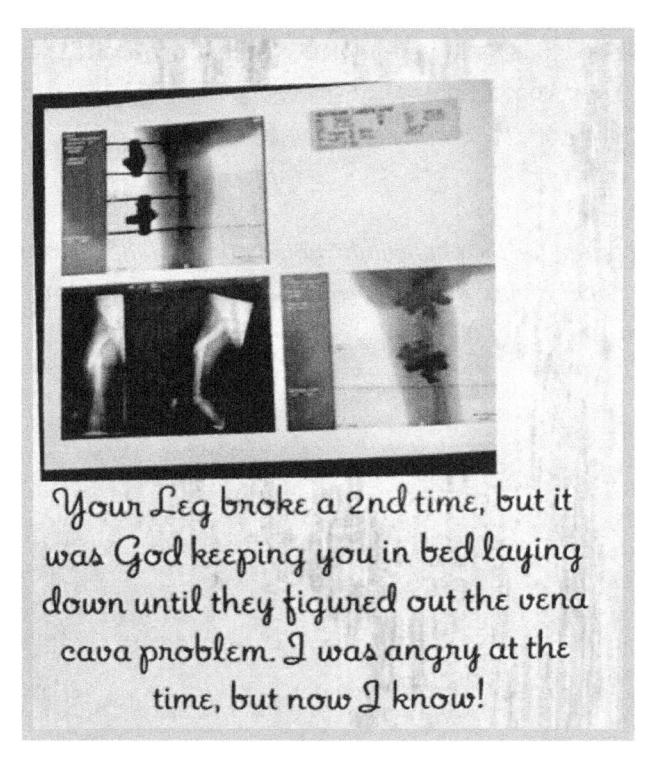

> *Your Leg broke a 2nd time, but it was God keeping you in bed laying down until they figured out the vena cava problem. I was angry at the time, but now I know!*

A page from the scrapbook I made that shows Landen's leg x-rays

Finally, this grueling experience was over, and Landen's healing could progress. There would be no more searching for answers. Although Landen still had a long road to recovery, we knew the next steps were imminent, making the wait more bearable. It felt like a heavy burden had been lifted off my shoulders.

I apologized to Dr. Linden for my previous treatment towards him, and he graciously accepted, comprehending that my sole concern was finding answers for Landen. He exited the room, and I held Landen tightly, expressing gratitude to God for introducing Dr. Linden into our lives at the perfect moment. I realized that God's timing is always impeccable.

We slept well that night, knowing Landen's journey would be filled with healing and strength, and that his future would be brimming with joy.

KARI HOFFMANN

"I will give thanks to you, LORD, with all my heart; I will tell of all Your wonderful deeds."

— PSALM 9:1 NIV

Lord, thank You for the opportunity to tell others of the amazing things You have done! Please help people to see how wonderful You are and how much You love them.

Chapter 32

The Sun Is Still Shining

As the sun rose on a new day, its radiant colors painted the sky, and I couldn't help but feel a sense of renewal and hope. Landen looked so much better. His skin color had improved, and I could see the transformation.

However, because of the twisted intestine, he had a new tube down his nose, and he wasn't allowed to drink anything. It was difficult for him to understand why he couldn't have ice chips or swallow water while he brushed his teeth. Watching him struggle broke my heart.

He became upset about not being able to drink—to the point where he didn't want any visitors, not even his grandparents. I respected his wishes and let him set the rules. We wrote his rules on the whiteboard: 1. No drinks or food allowed. 2. If visitors come, they have to play instead of just sitting around.

He fidgeted, trying to find comfort. It was strange to witness his restlessness, as he was before all the vomiting. When he was so sick, he would lie still and indifferent. But now, he had a newfound energy, a sign of progress.

Good news arrived. His chest tube had almost completely dried up, and only a small amount came out that morning. This meant we could remove those drains from his body—I couldn't wait to bid them goodbye forever.

The next day, the medical team let Landen try drinks to see if he could tolerate them. We watched the clock every hour, hoping he could manage 15 milliliters of fluid. If he tolerated it, then they would remove the tube.

Finally, his nose tube came out. The stomach drain would remain in but be kept clamped for a day to ensure it would remain dry. The doctors slowly fed his stomach to see if he could tolerate it. It was a slow process, as Landen's body had endured so much trauma. Now, he had to find his way back to normal function.

His pain was intense, with the drain wounds and the deep, gruesome belly wound. The wound doctors came every day to dress it, and I shielded our eyes with a blanket. To help ease the pain during dressing changes, they would give him laughing gas, and we found comfort in the company of the delightful nurse who administered it. His name was Cary, but we called him "Laughing Gas Cary." We always looked forward to his stories and jokes, distracting us from the painful procedures.

Another thing that made it bearable was when Dave got us flavored chapsticks as a way to add flavor to the laughing gas mask. Landen's favorite flavors were root beer and cherry coke. He and Haley would guess the flavor by closing their eyes and smelling. This was one of our favorite games.

Now that it was summer, Haley started visiting us. She brought joy and distraction to Landen, hanging out in his bed, watching shows, playing games, and participating in his therapy sessions. Even when she wasn't physically present, she would FaceTime us and keep her iPad in the corner of her room, allowing us to be part of her activities.

Dave and Haden kept busy with baseball and spending time with Courtney and Steve's boys, who are our cousins and neighbors. They also visited the hospital almost daily, although not for the entire day like Haley did.

This was our life for now, but at least we were together, united in our knowledge that we would go home soon.

After a busy day of playing, bedtime seemed like a breeze, but a frightening setback that night left me reeling.

During the night, the attending doctor checked on us periodically. Half-awakened by hearing him move around the room, I noticed that he put Landen back on oxygen because he was grunting and struggling to breathe. It was alarming, but I couldn't fully comprehend what happened until morning.

After our usual 5:00 am X-ray, the attending doctor and his nurse entered our room and informed me that the fluid had returned to his left lung. I couldn't believe it. *It can't be true,* I thought. This revelation sucked all the air out of the room. I had to escape so I could catch my breath.

I texted Dr. Wahoff and pleaded for him to come soon. I also called Dave and told him I needed to leave the hospital for a little while, asking him to come down alone and speak with people to get to the bottom of this. I was adamant that it must be a mistake. I told Landen that Dave was coming to play with him while I went to Target for some new toys.

When Dave arrived, I asked him to call Dr. Singewald and arrange for another ink study to be done as soon as possible. We needed to figure this out, but I had to leave it in Dave's hands. Dave and I made a great team in situations like this. When I'd had enough, I could call him to take over, and he would do it flawlessly. He talked to everyone and got answers and solutions every time.

While I was gone, Dave kept me informed. I was so grateful to have Dave.

Dave kept Landen happy, playing games and taking him for a walk while I was gone. When I returned, Landen looked much happier and more comfortable than when I had left. They had removed a significant amount of fluid, which provided great relief.

As we went to bed, we didn't have concrete answers, and our sleep was interrupted due to the diuretics, which caused frequent urination. However, I was confident that this new fluid in the X-ray was not lymph. It simply couldn't be, and I refused to believe it.

The next day, it was confirmed that the fluid was only serous fluid.

Serous fluid is a type of fluid that can build up in the body after surgery. It can form a collection known as a "seroma," which is typically found near the surgical incision site. My understanding is that serous fluid is essentially the clear, watery part of blood, containing plasma and some lymphatic fluid. It accumulates in the "dead space" left after tissue removal during surgery.

So this was a normal reaction to surgery and nothing to be alarmed about. There was no indication that the major chyle leak was back—praise God!

> "Then Jesus said to the centurion, 'Go! Let it be done just as you believed it would.' And his servant was healed at that moment"
>
> — MATTHEW 8:13 NIV

God, thank You for giving us the gift of faith to help us in our time of need.

Chapter 33

Holding On

The next day, Landen was happy and asked Dave to come spend the day with him again. We were now at day 80 since the attack, and with Dave coming, I thought it was time for my first visit home. Even though I had ventured out of the hospital a few times to shop or move about town a little, actually going to our home without Landen felt strange. But since he wanted me to go, I saw it as a sign that it was time to start rebuilding our lives.

The idea of cleaning the house and organizing things before our return from the hospital sounded terrific. I couldn't wait to shower and pack some summer clothes. We arrived at the hospital in April, but it was still snowing, so all I had were warm clothes my mom had been washing for me and bringing back. However, the thought of returning home without Landen and not seeing him there made me feel unsure and emotional. Plus, I hadn't driven a car in 80 days, which added to my anxiety.

Being decisive, as always, Dave told me he would come to the hospital while leaving the twins with his mom, Sharon, at our house. We agreed that I would meet him downstairs and take the car home. As I drove, tears streamed down my face, but I focused on the road and kept my emotions in check.

Arriving home, Nana Sharon and the twins greeted me. Though everyone was excited, I felt shocked and unprepared to be home. Everything was still as we left it, with winter boots and coats in the back hall, Easter decorations, and baskets on the fireplace. It was overwhelming, and I couldn't handle the emotions. I quickly showered and packed some summer clothes before returning to the hospital. I wasn't ready to be at home without Landen.

Returning to the hospital, it felt like I was seeing Landen with fresh eyes. I noticed he had put on weight due to the tube feeding and looked completely different compared to the day we first arrived.

After the frightening setback with the additional fluid, we were once more progressing, and the doctors confirmed Landen could try eating fat-free foods since a fat-free diet was still recommended to help ensure that the chyle leak did not return. Landen was excited to eat and ordered fat-free pizza and watermelon. However, after not eating for many days, his taste buds were funny, and he didn't like anything.

We hoped that if he could tolerate food, we could avoid the swallow ink study the doctors were considering. We wanted him to enjoy food and heal, but for now, it was necessary to make sure he received proper nutrition through the nose tube. This was especially necessary when he vomited much of what he ate.

I was ready for a new plan of action. I didn't want to stay in the hospital for another month. I tried to put pressure on the doctors to find the final piece of the puzzle so that we could go home. They ordered an ultrasound of the veins in Landen's neck and an echo to check for a clot and understand why his face was highly puffy. They found nothing, and we still didn't know why he couldn't keep food down, or why he needed oxygen.

Haden, Dave, and Haley came to play and kept us busy. Landen loved it when all of us were together. We cheered him on as he took bites of food, encouraging and supporting him. We even got him to stand on the side of the bed with the PT nurse, which he enjoyed. It had been almost six weeks, and soon, we could remove the external fixator from his leg.

The doctors decided Landen needed to do a swallow test to

understand why he couldn't tolerate food without vomiting. The test involved swallowing a drink with dye and taking X-rays every hour to track the movement of the dye through his digestive system.

The test was long and exhausting, and the drink was disgusting, but the results were perfect. There was no reason to believe that his stomach was the issue. We just needed to be patient and give his body time to align and start working correctly. It was a moment of relief and comfort.

Each day, he kept getting better and stronger. He needed less oxygen and tolerated more food, and his leg X-ray looked good, allowing us to remove the cast. Dr. Halverson discussed moving us to Gillette the next week.

Everything was moving along, and we were getting closer to leaving the hospital. We just had to hold on a little longer.

"When I thought, 'My foot slips,' your steadfast love, O LORD, held me up"

— PSALM 94:18 ESV

"Now then, stand still and see this great thing the LORD is about to do before your eyes."

— 1 SAMUEL 12:16 NIV

God, thank You for holding us up when we are weak. When we feel like we cannot go on, You somehow step in and keep us standing, ensuring that we make it through to see the final victory. Help us to keep our eyes on You so that in the end, we will stand in Your great miracles and blessings.

Chapter 34

Nurse Heroes

On day 106, we found out we were getting discharged the following Monday to go to Gillette, a rehab facility. Although we weren't entirely out of the woods, moving to a rehab hospital was a huge victory! Landen had fought so hard, and now we could focus on continuing the healing process instead of fighting for his life.

On Sunday, my mom brought sheet cakes for all the doctors and nurses to express our gratitude. Nurses we loved came in to hug us, give us small gifts, and say goodbye. We made cards for everyone. I knew Monday would bring so many emotions. I couldn't believe it—we were leaving.

But there was one more thing I needed to do: it was time for me to meet the two nurses who had saved Landen's life.

I didn't want to be alone when I met them, so I called Lindsay, knowing she was a night owl. She came with her trusty Mountain Dew and sat with me as the nurses shared their stories.

One of the nurses, Jessica, shared that on that particular day, she and her colleagues had gone to the mall—something they never did together—to return an item. However, unlike the other stores, the specific store they needed wasn't open yet. So they decided to wait outside of that store, standing near the second-floor balcony railing.

That was when they witnessed Landen's freefall and heard my piercing screams.

Without hesitation, they rushed to his side and began performing CPR. "Landen wasn't breathing and had no heartbeat when we first reached him, but thankfully, we were able to revive him."

As I listened to the nurse's account of that fateful day, it became evident that her real-life job involved administering CPR when needed. She did this frequently and knew exactly what she was doing. Both nurses felt like God had placed them in the exact spot at the mall when we needed help the most. They believed that God had orchestrated everything, ensuring that they saw Landen as he was in freefall, while also hearing my desperate cries for help.

Hearing the nurses describe Landen as being medically deceased, a lump formed in my throat. This was something I had assumed, but did not know for sure—whether or not he had a heartbeat when they reached him. All I knew for sure is that after they started CPR, they called out "We have a heartbeat!" Up to this point, I had never heard anyone explicitly say that there was no heartbeat before the CPR.

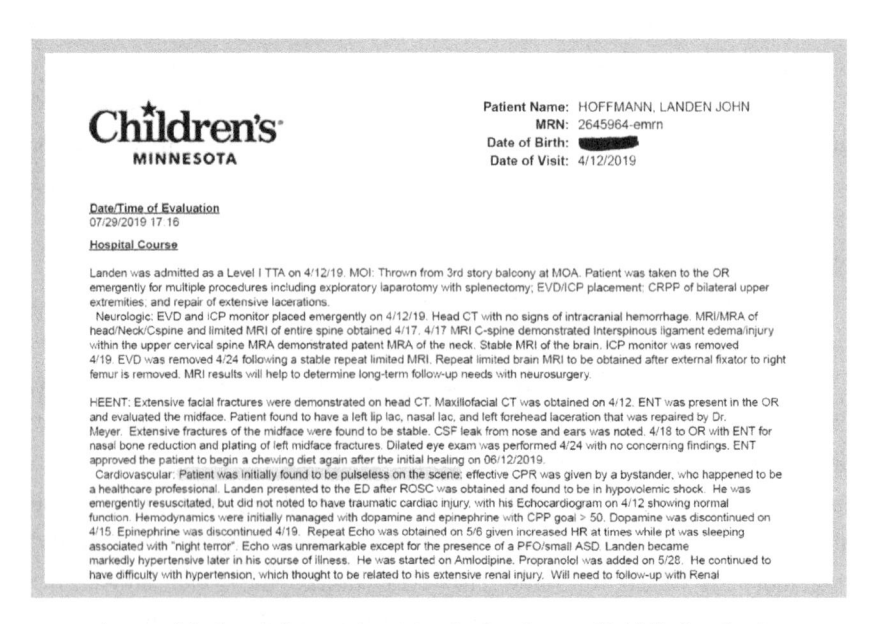

A scan of the hospital report that states that Landen was "initially found to be pulseless on the scene" by healthcare professionals

> HEENT: Extensive facial fractures were demonstrated on head CT. Maxillofa
> and evaluated the midface. Patient found to have a left lip lac, nasal lac, and
> Meyer. Extensive fractures of the midface were found to be stable. CSF lea
> nasal bone reduction and plating of left midface fractures. Dilated eye exam
> approved the patient to begin a chewing diet again after the initial healing or
>   Cardiovascular: Patient was initially found to be pulseless on the scene; ef
> a healthcare professional. Landen presented to the ED after ROSC was obt
> emergently resuscitated, but did not noted to have traumatic cardiac injury, \

Close up of the relevant portion of the hospital report

They continued sharing their memories, and hearing them describe what Landen looked like at that moment took my breath away. My memory was fragmented and darkened. While I remember urging him to breathe and pleading with people to pray, I did not personally recollect the state of his body. However, the nurses both remembered vividly that in addition to him not breathing and not having a heartbeat, Landen had broken bones sticking out of the skin in multiple places, and that there was a lot of blood.

Tears streamed down my face, and I trembled with emotion throughout the conversation. Lindsay was beside me, supporting and helping me absorb every word. I was profoundly grateful these two nurses wanted to meet us, embrace us, and share their perspectives.

How could I ever express enough gratitude to these two angels in disguise? Thank you, Jessica and Kimberly!

> Elisha summoned Gehazi and said, "Call the Shunammite." And he did. When she came, he said, "Take your son." She came in, fell at his feet and bowed to the ground. Then she took her son and went out.
>
> — 2 KINGS 4:36-37 NIV

> While Jesus was still speaking, someone came from the house of Jairus, the synagogue leader. "Your daughter is dead," he said. "Don't bother the teacher anymore."

Hearing this, Jesus said to Jairus, "Don't be afraid; just believe, and she will be healed."

When he arrived at the house of Jairus, he did not let anyone go in with him except Peter, John and James, and the child's father and mother. Meanwhile, all the people were wailing and mourning for her. "Stop wailing," Jesus said. "She is not dead but asleep."

They laughed at him, knowing that she was dead. But he took her by the hand and said, "My child, get up!" Her spirit returned, and at once she stood up. Then Jesus told them to give her something to eat. Her parents were astonished.

— LUKE 8:49-56 NIV

Thank You for putting these nurses in the right place at the right time. Thank You, Jesus, for giving me back my son!

Chapter 35

Freedom

On the day we left the hospital, the music therapy teacher arrived and sang a beautiful farewell song she had written to the tune of "In the Jungle." She affectionately called it "In the PICU." I couldn't help but tear up as she performed, realizing the significance of this moment.

We had been through so much in this place. Here is a hospital report showing a list of all the procedures Landen went through at Children's.

> **Hospital procedures:**
>
> 04/12/2019: exploratory laparotomy with splenectomy by Dr. ▓▓▓ and Dr. ▓▓▓
> 04/12/2019: layered repair of 4cm left forehead laceration, simple repair of right intranasal laceration, examination of oral cavity, nose and ears under anesthesia and repair of left upper lip laceration by Dr. ▓▓▓ and Dr. ▓▓▓
> 04/12/2019: closed reduction and splinting of right mid-femur fracture with J-splint, closed reduction and percutaneous pinning of right supracondylar elbow fracture with irrigation and debridement of grade 2 open fracture with closure of wound, closed treatment of ulnar shaft fracture, open reduction with percutaneous fixation of left supracondylar elbow fracture with irrigation and debridement of the open fracture, closed reduction and splinting of left both-bone forearm fracture with irrigation and debridement of open wound, and closed treatment of pubic ramus fracture by Dr. ▓▓▓.
> 04/12/2019: placement of right frontal external ventricular drainage catheter and right frontal intracranial pressure monitor by Dr. ▓▓▓
> 04/18/2019: open reduction and internal fixation of left midface fractures and closed reduction of nasal bone fracture by Dr. ▓▓▓ and Dr. ▓▓▓
> 04/30/2019: fabrication of right femur fracture spica orthosis with re-application of right femur fracture trauma J-splint after mold application and exam under anesthesia with imaging of right elbow, left elbow and left forearm by Dr. ▓▓▓
> 04/30/2019: insertion of right 8.5 Fr pig tail chest tube and NJ tube placement with fluoroscopic guidance by Dr. ▓▓▓
> 04/30/2019: examination under anesthesia of bilateral upper extremities, removal of k wires from bilateral upper extremities and placement of left wrist brace by Dr. ▓▓▓.
> 05/15/2019: exploratory right thoracoscopy followed by right thoracotomy with pleurectomy and ligation of chylous leak. Placement of 20 F right chest tube.
> 05/16/2019: abdominal drain placed per Interventional radiology. NJ placed
> 05/30/2019: External fixation to RLE femur Fx. with Dr. ▓▓▓
> 06/10/2019: MRI guided lymphoscintigraphy with IR
> 06/12/2019: Laparoscopy converted to laparotomy with lysis of adhesions and ligation of peripancreatic chyle leak by Dr. ▓▓▓
> 06/15/2019: insertion of 8.5 Fr left sided pig tail chest tube under sedation by Dr. ▓▓▓, and placement of purse-string suture around existing right sided chest tube by Dr. ▓▓▓
> 06/15/2019: Left tube thoracostomy, Exploratory Laparotomy with repair of gastric perforation with Dr. ▓▓▓ and Dr. ▓▓▓
> 06/21/2019: US guided drainage of RUQ fluid with accordion drain placement - Dr. ▓▓▓
> 06/21/2019: Right heart catheterization. Angiography. Stent placement in IVC - Dr. Rios IV and Dr. ▓▓▓
> 7/22/2019: Intraoperative debridement of abdominal wound with Dr. ▓▓▓ plastic surgery. Placement of stem cell dressing and replacement of wound VAC.

A list of all the surgeries and procedures Landen had at Children's Hospital of Minnesota (with doctors names redacted).

Even now, it seems surreal that God brought him safely and securely through so many serious injuries and complications.

As the music teacher sang that morning, Landen seemed shy, his emotions swirling beneath the surface, and I could sense his nervousness. Dave lovingly covered his head with one of his blankets, providing comfort.

Dr. Fugate, the PICU doctor, entered our room before we left and said, "We fought a good battle. Landen is a strong young man. But I do want to warn you that he will experience withdrawal symptoms from all the pain medication, which was way more than a grown man could handle."

I didn't fully understand at that moment; I was just focused on getting out of there.

The hospital arranged an ambulance to transport Landen, and Dr.

MIRACLE AT THE MALL

Fugate informed us that Landen would keep the NG (feeding) tube in until we arrived at Gillette, where they would remove it.

The ambulance drivers came to greet us and asked what brought him to Children's, unaware of who he was.

He said, "I fell over the balcony at the mall."

I could see the shock immediately register on their faces; they had heard the story. "Well, Landen, you look great! We're glad we get the chance to drive you around today."

Landen still didn't know he was thrown, and we were waiting for the right time to tell him.

With the sirens blaring and lights flashing, we got into the back of the ambulance. I rode with him this time while Dave followed us in his car. Landen didn't like the sirens because they hurt his ears, but he enjoyed seeing the lights.

When we arrived at Gillette, it felt like we were checking into a hotel. There was a beautiful welcome desk, and we were quickly taken to his room. It was much bigger than his previous one, and a fresh blanket awaited him. It gave us such a good feeling, knowing that this was where he would finish healing—where he would learn to walk, eat, and then eventually go home. How exciting!

Right away, we met new nurses and a doctor who would be following his progress. There would be no more teams of people outside the door every morning trying to devise action plans. I explained how I didn't like Landen being force-fed through the NG tube. I showed them a picture of him before we came to Children's and another picture of him during our time there. The difference was astonishing—he looked like a completely different kid. The doctor agreed with me; there would be no more force-feeds. It was time to get that tube out of his nose.

I couldn't believe it when the nurse said all she needed to do was pull the tube out. I thought, *No way will it come out easily after being in there for over 100 days. How will that feel?* But Landen wanted it out, so we counted down from three, and the nurse pulled. It wasn't easy at all—it was long, gross, and painful. Landen screamed, cried, and got mad. We didn't expect that reaction, but he quickly cheered up once it was finally out.

What a relief it was to have everything detached from him, except for the wound vac on his stomach. It felt like freedom, but I was hesitant because it was unfamiliar. We spent the rest of the day exploring and meeting people. It was a strange feeling not having someone checking his stats every hour. I even pressed the nurse button to ensure they didn't need to check anything.

We were given a daily schedule of rehab sessions. Suddenly, Landen would be a busy boy, almost like going to school. It was a new routine to get used to, but it meant progress and healing.

After we settled in, they asked Landen if he would like a bath. Of course, he said, "Yes!"

They came to pick him up in a sling chair and lowered it into the bathtub, carefully keeping the wound vac dry. Then, they poured in loads of bubbles and water toys. It was like a dream come true. We finally got to wash his hair correctly and clean him up. We were both so happy.

We wheeled back to the room and put on new, fresh pajamas Lindsay had brought as a welcome-home gift. It was so easy to wear actual pajamas now, with only the wound vac cord to worry about. That night, after they gave him melatonin, he fell asleep peacefully with the scent of clean soap in the air.

The plans of the enemy have been canceled.

"Though I walk in the midst of trouble, you preserve my life; you stretch out your hand against the wrath of my enemies, and your right hand delivers me."

— PSALMS 138:7 ESV

God, we know that You are more powerful than any adversary we face. We trust in You to rescue us and deliver us!

Chapter 36

The Trial Is Over

LANDEN'S HEALING STARTED TO FEEL MORE REAL. I BELIEVED THE leak wouldn't come back, and Dr. Wahoff gave us the green light so Landen could eat whatever he wanted. It was humbling to realize that eating is one of life's greatest joys—one we take for granted until it's taken away.

Landen got to have authentic pizza! It was a small step, but it meant so much.

Soon, we would try walking, and I couldn't wait. We had one more X-ray, and if Dr. Engles gave us the go-ahead, Landen would be walking. He could stand with help, and they brought us a standing wheelchair, which was super fun for a kid to ride around in.

In Gillette, we could get day passes to leave for a few hours and return, so we decided to see a movie together as a family. Dave took the bus with Landen because of his wound vac and wheelchair, and I drove with Haden and Haley. It was surreal, with our whole family out together at a movie. We all got *The Lion King* popcorn buckets and enjoyed the film together. It felt so right, and I wished I could freeze time.

When we got back, they informed us Landen was doing

exceptionally well with his therapies, and we might even be looking at discharge the next week. It had only been eight days since we arrived at Gillette, so I tried not to get my hopes up. The idea of leaving so soon seemed too good to be true. I wondered how he could learn to walk that quickly.

Landen had an X-ray of his chest to ensure the fluid was still gone, and also one of his femur to ensure it was healing properly. He'd had countless X-rays in the hospital, and most of them were scary and even painful. However, he laughed and had fun with the technicians during these X-rays. I cried joyfully because this was the first happy X-ray, a sign that everything was falling into place in his body.

We were now convinced that we were finally done with this ordeal. The major trials and tribulations were now over. Dr. Wahoff visited us in our room when we returned and pulled up the chest photo, showing us its clarity and signifying that everything looked great!

I couldn't help but exclaim, "Amen!" and then gave Dr. Wahoff a heartfelt hug.

He was genuinely happy to deliver this news, as he had been fighting alongside us throughout this entire journey.

Next up was Dr. Engles, who took a little longer to review the images since he wasn't at Gillette. We had to wait until our physical therapy session to find out if this would be the day Landen started walking.

As we left for physical therapy in the standing wheelchair, we were filled with anticipation and excitement. When we arrived at the gym, the teacher informed us that Landen would be attempting to walk. It was an exciting moment, but she brought us back to earth, reminding us it wouldn't be easy. She took a belt and buckled it around his waist, holding onto a leash-type attachment to keep him steady.

She guided Landen to stand up and take a step, but it was challenging. He almost lost his balance. He tried again, and this time, they set up baseball bases for him to make it to each one. He had a wobbly limp, and it was tough. He didn't enjoy it and ended up crying, wanting to quit. I cried, too, because I didn't realize how difficult it would be.

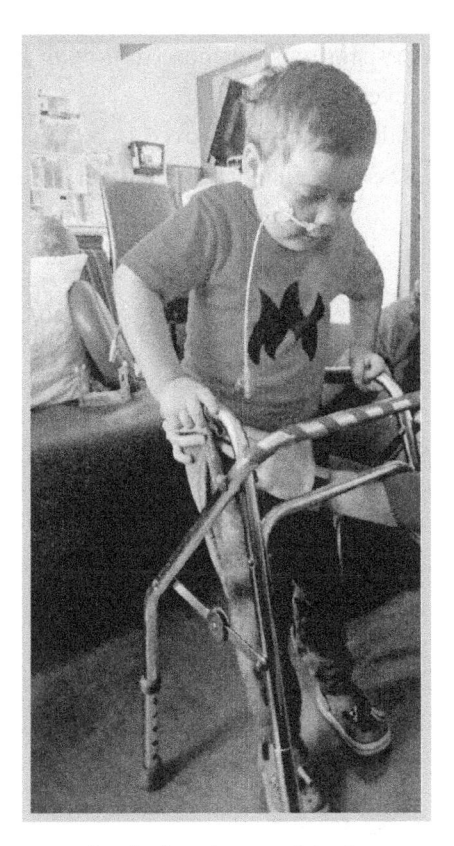

Landen learning to walk again

I spoke to Dr. Engles on the phone, and he explained that when a person breaks a bone like a femur and doesn't use it for a while, it may be a different length than the other leg until the person starts using it again. Eventually, it would equal out. He suggested putting a lift in Landen's shoe to help.

In those final days leading up to our expected discharge, frustration started to creep in, and I knew I needed to step back and gather myself. The doctors told us we could leave the hospital within the next two days, so I asked Dave to take over Landen's therapies during that time. I recognized that he would push Landen to succeed whereas I, overcome with emotions, would likely be overwhelmed and in tears, and more likely to opt for his comfort at times when he needed to be pushed. While Dave spent most of those days with Landen, I returned to sleep by his side every night.

My belief in Landen's progress proved to be true. Dave was terrific during the therapy sessions, encouraging and pushing Landen to do his best. He got Landen to walk and smile, and during one of my trips to the grocery store, he sent me a video of Landen hitting a softball with a foam bat and then quickly walking the bases, cheered on by everyone around him. Yes, his steps were still wobbly, but the fact that he was walking meant the world to us.

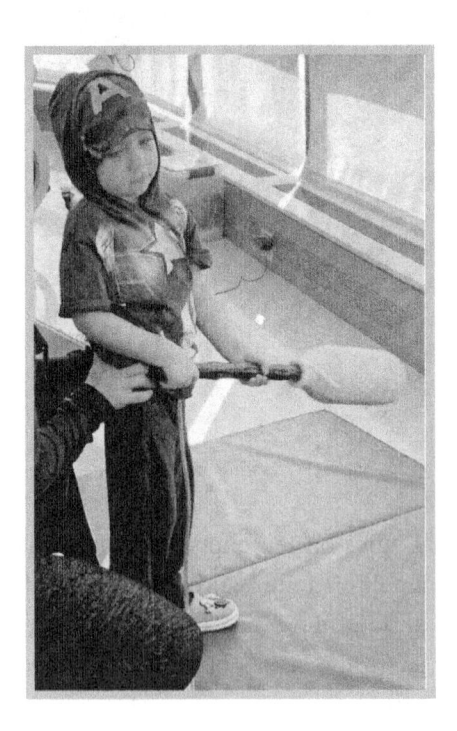

We had a discharge meeting, outlining what we needed to do once we got home. We would continue PT twice a week and make appointments with the various doctors still following up with Landen —six doctors in all. We also needed to be diligent in taking medicines on schedule.

However, the biggest challenge was his belly wound. It was deep and unpleasant. Whenever it was time for dressing changes, I couldn't bring myself to look at it. Open cuts and blood always made me cringe, causing me immense discomfort.

Dr. Wahoff and Dr. Loake presented me with two options: either I could bring Landen to the clinic every day to have the wound cleaned, packed, and bandaged, or I could learn to do it myself. All I desired was to be home, so despite my aversion to such sights, I made the difficult decision to learn.

They patiently showed me the process—removing the bandage and gauze, applying ointment, soaking the new gauze in a solution, and then gently packing the wound with the clean gauze before covering it again. They gave me a generous supply of materials and a medical supply phone number to call for regular deliveries. I was determined to do whatever it took to ensure the wound healed correctly. The last thing I wanted to do was drive back to the hospital every day. I wanted to go home and stay home!

After Dave packed up the car with our belongings, I remained at Gillette for one final discharge meeting and to say goodbye to the fantastic staff who had cared for us. This time, bidding farewell was easier since our stay had been shorter, only two weeks.

"Okay, Landen, it's over," I whispered, taking a deep breath and mustering my strength. I removed from our door a sign someone had made for Landen, which said, "GO Landen GO!" Holding the sign and two "Welcome Home" balloons tightly in my hand, I picked him up and put him on my hip. With a surge of emotion, I carried Landen to the car.

It felt magical.

"Let's go home!"

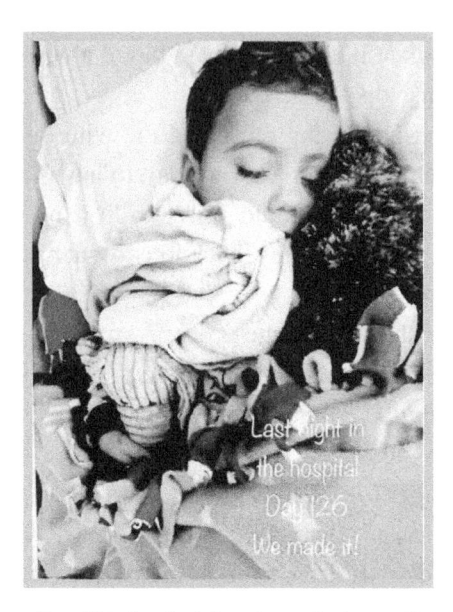

Day 126: Landen's last day in the hospital!

    Whenever we are going through trials, we must recognize that they will come to an end. Sometimes it feels like the trials will never end, but that's just our emotions misleading us. We know that the trials will pass, and we will see our day of victory and celebration. We must keep that day in mind and hold it in our hearts until we see it come to pass.

> "You have turned my mourning into joyful dancing. You have taken away my clothes of mourning and clothed me with joy, that I might sing praises to you and not be silent. O LORD my God, I will give you thanks forever!"
>
> — PSALM 30:11-12 NLT

> "But for you who fear My name, the sun of righteousness will rise with healing in its wings, and you will go out and leap like calves from the stall."
>
> — MALACHI 4:2 ESV

Lord, for anyone still going through a trial, I pray that you give them a picture in their heart of the day they will leap for joy. Help them to worship their way through, and turn their mourning into dancing, in Jesus name, amen.

Chapter 37

Not All Angels Have Wings

"You are the God who works wonders; you have made known your might among the peoples."

— Psalm 77:14 ESV

"Jesus said, 'This sickness will not end in death. No, it is for God's glory so that God's Son may be glorified through it'."

— John 11:4 ESV

When we finally came home on August 17th, 2019, after spending 127 days in the hospital, I knew that I needed to do something to honor and thank all the incredible individuals who played a part in saving my son's life. From the first responders to the civilians, nurses, and doctors, everyone was a hero in our eyes. God placed them in our path with a divine purpose, whether they knew it or not. Some may have already known Christ and answered His call to help Landen, while God placed others there without them even realizing why.

Every person we encountered during those 127 days was meant to be there for a reason. They were there to teach me something, show me something, or directly contribute to Landen's healing through surgeries, therapies, or other forms of care. Every person was necessary, and Landen and I cherished and loved them deeply.

Even the accidents and setbacks that occurred, like the stomach puncture that required another surgery, happened for a purpose. Setbacks don't matter when it comes to healing because God is the ultimate Healer. Sometimes, we have to experience the worst outcomes before we can truly appreciate the magnitude of the miracle God has in store for us.

When everyone returned to school in the fall, I knew I needed to keep myself busy and find a way to thank the people who deserved it. I met with lawyers to discuss making the mall safer and ensuring that aggressive individuals like the perpetrator would not be allowed back into public places like the mall.

I would come to find out that the mall authorities had previously issued a trespass to the man who did this to Landen, preventing him from stepping foot onto the mall property, but that under the law, the trespass could only be temporary. This meant we would need to advocate for changes to local ordinances which would enable businesses to enact lifetime trespasses on perpetrators. Before this, they could only trespass criminals for up to one year.

We were able to successfully advocate with local city leadership for a change to the city ordinance which would allow businesses to trespass individuals for longer periods of time. This was a huge win for all involved. It's my understanding that the man who attacked Landen has now received a lifetime trespass from the mall property. The mall has also implemented changes to strengthen security protocols. So God brought good from this terrible act in many different ways.

Shortly after we came home, we experienced another unexpected blessing. Wes Walz, who is a former player and current television analyst for the Minnesota Wild, lives in our hometown of Woodbury. Somehow Wes got my phone number. He had heard how that we were huge fans of the Wild and he personally invited us to a game, offering us our own suite at the rink!

We had been to Minnesota Wild games before, but this time, the excitement was different. It wasn't just about going to a hockey game —it was about celebrating how far Landen had come. We were able to invite 20 people to join us, making it a joyful gathering of family and friends.

Landen with Wes Walz (left). Landen, siblings, and cousins, pose with Minnesota Wild mascot, Nordy, in the suite they gave us (right)

After the game, our family of five was invited down to the locker room to meet some of the players—and to see Zach again. This time, it wasn't in a hospital room filled with worry. It was at the arena, surrounded by life and light. Zach was just as happy to see us as we were to see him. When we asked for a picture, he smiled and said, "Hold on, let me get Alisha—she'll want to be in it too." That simple gesture filled my heart with overwhelming gratitude and brought tears to my eyes.

We took a beautiful photo together, this time knowing that Landen was okay and that we were back to living, truly living. I'm so thankful

I said yes to Zach's visit on that awful day because the memories we created—both in that hospital room and at the arena—are ones we will cherish forever. Moments like those remind me what life is all about: connection, kindness, and the unexpected gifts that come when we decide to say yes to opportunities.

Zach Parise and his wife, Alisha, posing for a photo with our family

There was one other very notable event that took place shortly after Landen was able to go back home, perhaps the most important one. I wanted to bring all the fantastic heroes from the hospital together in one place to witness Landen, who was out of the hospital and thriving. I wanted them to see firsthand the miracle they had played a part in. So, I contacted every one of them, whether by finding their names in the police report or through personal connections at the hospital. I created a list of all these incredible individuals who had become a part of our story. I then planned a party, which we called the "PERFECT Celebration Party."

Photos from the PERFECT Celebration Party. Upper left: Dr. Engels holding Landen. Upper middle: Me and Landen. Upper right: Our family. Lower left: Brian (my cousin who is a trauma surgeon) along with his daughter, Esther, and Landen. Lower right: Katie, Courtney, and Lindsay

We rented two party rooms and had food catered. We had wait staff to attend to everyone's needs and provided name tags to quickly identify and recognize each person and their role in our journey. We placed signs around the rooms, such as "Not all angels wear wings. Some wear scrubs."

In the Bible, angels are often shown to be heroes, warriors, protectors, and rescuers. We couldn't think of a better metaphor for the people who helped Landen.

In one of the rooms, we displayed a massive poster of Landen on day one of being in the hospital, holding his puppy under his broken arm, covered in casts. The poster had the verse, "You intended to harm me, but God intended it all for good. He brought me to this position so I could save the lives of many people" (Genesis 50:20 NLT). Katie, my cousin, ensured that every "angel" who attended the party signed the poster, forever commemorating their presence in our lives.

The night of the party was genuinely remarkable. We hugged, told stories, and expressed our gratitude to all these "angels" who had played a part in Landen's healing. We had a slideshow playing in one of the rooms, showcasing Landen's journey in the hospital and all the significant moments. Meanwhile, Landen and Will, the boy who had been with us that day at the mall, ran around the rooms, having fun, playing games, and simply enjoying themselves. Landen took pictures with each person and thanked them for their role in his journey.

Landen (left) with his best friend Will (right) who was with us at the mall that day

One person who stood out was the female police officer who drove me to the hospital on that fateful day. She cried throughout the party, and I knew God was showing her something powerful that night. Many of the surgeons and doctors who attended had tears in their eyes as they watched Landen running and playing.

Everyone was in awe of the miracle they had witnessed.

REQUEST FROM THE PUBLISHER:

If you enjoyed this book and believe that Kari's account of God's miracle at the mall is a story worth spreading, will you please take a minute or two and leave a review for Kari's book on Amazon? Leaving reviews online—especially on Amazon—is a great way to help us spread the message.

We are hoping that the book will do well enough for us to be able to have the story made into a movie! Thank you for helping us spread the word about Kari's book. God bless you!

Afterword

Our first night at home under one roof was pure happiness, but many challenges still lay ahead for us.

We gathered on the couch that night, watched *The Lion King* together again, and ordered Chinese food. It felt so comforting and loving to be reunited as a family. Landen enjoyed a long, soothing bath before bedtime and wanted to sleep in his bed, which was a beautiful moment. I placed his old baby monitor in his room and recorded a video of him peacefully sleeping, capturing the joy and relief that filled my heart. Our home was filled with peace and contentment as we drifted off to sleep under one roof.

In the following days, people all over the world were celebrating Landen's miraculous recovery. There were more news reports, prayer groups celebrating the victory, and viral social media posts. God was working through Landen's story and there was certainly a lot to celebrate!

Afterword

> **Franklin Graham** ✓
> November 25, 2019
>
> Here's some good news for a Monday morning. Do you remember Landen Hoffman? He's the 5-year-old boy who was thrown from a third-floor balcony in the Mall ▓▓▓▓▓ in Minnesota back in April. Well, after 15 medical procedures and surgeries, Landen is now walking, doing well, and enjoying kindergarten! That's a huge praise to God! The update said, "Landen loves life and Jesus!" He tells people when they get hurt, "I fell off a cliff, but angels caught me and Jesus loves me, so I'm ok and you will be too!" Even at such a young age, Landen's testimony and faith are touching many—great job Landen!
>
> The Word of God says, "Truly, I say to you, whoever does not receive the kingdom of God like a child shall not enter it" (Luke 18:17).
>
> FOXNEWS.COM
> **Boy, 5, thrown from Mall of America balcony is 'walking perfectly,' family says**
> The 5-year-old boy who survived after he was thrown from a Mall of America third-floor balco...
>
> 👍❤ Felecia Gilliam, Karen Ruhl and 165K others   14.5K comments   34K shares

But for us, we were mainly focused on trying to establish a new routine and find some normalcy. The start of kindergarten was only two weeks away, and I was determined to send Landen to school despite the difficulties. His teacher came to our house to meet and get an understanding of his needs. We explained that Landen could not sit on the floor and get up independently and needed to walk slower than the other children. Additionally, we mentioned that he would require frequent breaks and visits to the nurse for his belly wound and bandage checks.

I feared I was rushing him back into everyday life too quickly, but I didn't want his traumatic experience to rob him of going through kindergarten. It was a challenging time for both of us. He cried frequently and longed for my presence, and I felt the same way. We had become accustomed to being together 24/7, making it difficult for us to be apart.

To provide him with some comfort, I sent him to school with a few tiny treasures from the hospital, hoping they would give him a sense of security. The school allowed him to call me from the nurse's office twice daily. Yet, despite these efforts, he still struggled with anger, outbursts, and tearfulness. This was in part due to narcotic withdrawal, which Dr. Fugate explained could take a long time, potentially even years, to recover from fully.

Adjusting to the world became the most challenging part for him. Before the attack, Landen was the kindest and happiest boy, adored by his teachers for his gentle and sweet nature. But now, his kindergarten teacher had begun to call me, expressing concerns about him hitting another child and being difficult in class. I vividly remember one day during dismissal when he loudly yelled out to his teacher that he needed to use the bathroom—something he would have never done before his injuries.

Witnessing this transformation in him shook me to my core. It felt like another trial in life, and even my family, though supportive, shared my fears. We had no idea how long it would take for Landen to fully get back to his previous self.

Landen continued to act in ways that were entirely out of character, and I found myself constantly worried, scared, and saddened. This pattern continued for the next three years. Landen wasn't the same, and I was far from okay. I found myself constantly asking God to help me teach him obedience, selflessness, and kindness all over again. Although I would catch glimpses of the real Landen from time to time, the journey was long and challenging.

During this time, I sought functional doctors to help us restore Landen to his true self. Though these efforts helped, I understood there were no quick fixes. It all required time. Patience became a virtue I needed to learn, as I had always tried to rush through things as quickly as possible.

Afterword

This traumatic experience truly changed me. I have become more carefree about the little things, taking the time to truly listen to my body and not push myself or Landen when we aren't ready. I find solace in prayer, constantly speaking to God in my mind throughout the day and asking for guidance. I worry less now, knowing that worrying does not bring us closer to our goals; it only makes the journey more difficult.

I enjoy every sunrise and sunset, understanding that tomorrow is never promised. I love and appreciate my family wholeheartedly. I have learned not to try to change them but rather to cast my cares on God regarding any problems or difficulties they may have. I have witnessed the immense power of prayer and the act of asking God for what we need and thanking Him for all He has done.

I also look back in awe of my extended family and how they rallied around us in prayer and support when we needed them most. After this experience, I feel more gratitude and appreciation for them than ever before.

Front row (L to R): Caleb and Olive (my nephew and niece) Second row: (L to R): Whitney and Kaia (nieces), Kathy (my mom) and Steve (my dad), Landen. Back row (L to R): Jared (my brother-in-law) and Mandy (sister), Me and Dave, Kristi (sister-in-law) and Matt (brother), Haden and Haley

Afterword

Jesus loves us, and we are all His Creation—the work of His hands. There is no greater love than the love He showed us by dying on a cross for our sins. Simply being in His presence, whether sitting at His feet with worship music or basking in His love, brings renewal and strength to overcome anything. While not everyone in the world may have our best interests at heart, I have realized there are more good people than evil, and those who may seem lost are simply trying to find their place in this world, just like Jesus' lost sheep.

Today, nearly five years after that miraculous day, I can confidently say I have Landen back wholly. He looks like himself again, displays his kind and loving heart, and has reclaimed his true nature. It was a long and arduous journey to learn the lessons God was trying to teach me about humility, love, and patience, but I believe I have finally reached that point. I am so grateful to the world for praying for us during our darkest times. With you, we were able to recover. The power of prayer truly works.

Afterword

Today, Landen is completely healed and whole. He loves playing hockey!

Last Easter, we shared our story at the church where I grew up and also at the church we now attend. These experiences marked significant milestones in our healing journey. Landen and I shared our testimony, and the relief was indescribable. After listening to our story that day, God saved the souls of thousands of people who responded to the invitation to give their lives to Christ. Approximately 3,700 people indicated that they made decisions for Christ that day!

God is so good! He's using this tragic situation to bring people into His Kingdom, and hopefully to encourage, strengthen, and inspire many others.

Landen loves sharing how God saved him. He is open and passionate, doing everything in his power to win the souls of his friends. He prays with them and tells them about how God saved him

Afterword

and loves every one of us. He encourages them to choose love over hate, saying, "If you're my friend, I hope you choose love."

If his friends choose otherwise, he reminds them that the choice is theirs, but at least he told them who God is. From there, it is up to them to decide whether to follow Him. I admire Landen's bravery and boldness regarding his love for Christ.

Over the years, we've poured our hearts into finding strength, growing, and making progress every step of the way. We've experienced highs and lows, celebrated triumphs, and faced setbacks. However, we emerged more robust and resilient through it all. Now, I feel ready and compelled to share our incredible story of healing with the world.

As I write this miracle in story form, I'm reminded of all the emotions, experiences, and lessons we've learned. Our story can inspire others who are going through similar struggles. It will serve as a beacon of hope, reminding them that miracles can happen, healing is possible, and the power of faith and gratitude can lead to extraordinary transformations.

To all the readers out there, I want to convey the heartfelt message that miracles, indeed, still happen. Our story is a testament to the power of God and how He can bring about incredible transformations. God has purposes that prevail no matter the circumstances, and when we put our faith in Him, we find the strength to overcome darkness and evil.

We found solace and strength in the mighty name of Jesus, and through our faith and belief, we witnessed the miraculous. I hope you carry this profound truth in your heart and remember it always. When faced with challenges, remember the power of God and the name of Jesus. You can triumph over adversity with God as your anchor and Jesus as your guide.

Let our story be a source of inspiration and a reminder that God will always emerge victorious. May you accept this truth and let it guide your journey through the trials of life. Miracles are possible, and with Jesus, you can overcome anything.

About the Author

Kari Hoffmann is a loving wife and mother, and a woman of strong Christian faith. She was thrust into the spotlight when the story about her son Landen received worldwide media coverage. Kari loves sharing her testimony and is available for media interviews and speaking engagements. Please contact: karimediarequests@gmail.com to book Kari for interviews or speaking engagements.

Made in the USA
Monee, IL
12 May 2025